The Space Between the Notes

The Space Between the Notes examines a series of relationships central to sixties counter-culture: psychedelic coding and rock music, the Rolling Stones and Charlie Manson, the Beatles and the 'Summer of Love', Jimi Hendrix and hallucinogenics, Pink Floyd and space rock. Sheila Whiteley combines musicology and socio-cultural analysis to illuminate this terrain, illustrating her argument with key recordings of the time: Cream's *She Walks Like a Bearded Rainbow*, Hendrix's *Purple Haze*, Pink Floyd's *Astronomy Dominé* and Procul Harum's *A Whiter Shade of Pale*, among others.

The appropriation of progressive rock by young, urban dance bands in the 1990s make this study of sixties and seventies counter-culture a lively intervention. It will inform students of popular music and culture, and spark off recognition and interest from those who lived through the period, as well as for a new generation who draw inspiration from its iconography and sensibilities today.

'This is the most sustained attempt yet to explore the complexities and paradoxes of psychedelic music and progressive rock. The strength of Sheila Whiteley's approach lies in her expertise in both musicological and cultural analysis. . . . Her concept of "psychedelic coding" is sure to prove of immense value to future researchers in the field.'

Dave Laing

Sheila Whiteley is a Senior Lecturer in popular music at Salford College of Technology, Manchester, and a part-time tutor for the Open University.

The Space Between the Notes

Rock and the counter-culture

Sheila Whiteley

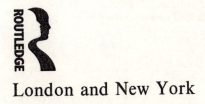

London and New York

First published 1992
by Routledge
11 New Fetter Lane, London EC4P 4EE

Simultaneously published in the USA and Canada
by Routledge
a division of Routledge, Chapman and Hall Inc.
29 West 35th Street, New York, NY 10001

Set in 10/12pt Times by Witwell Ltd
Printd and bound in Great Britain by
TJ Press (Padstow) Ltd, Padstow, Cornwall

British Library Cataloguing-in-Publication Data
Whiteley, Sheila
  The space between the notes.
  1. Rock music. Sociology
  I. Title
  306.484

Library of Congress Cataloging-in-Publication Data
Whiteley, Sheila
  The space between the notes: rock and the counter-culture/
  Sheila Whiteley.
  p.   cm.
  Includes bibliographical references and index.
  1. Rock music—1961—1970—History and criticism. 2. Rock
  music—1971—1980—History and criticism. 3. Popular culture.
  I. Title.
  ML3534.W555 1992   91–3646
  781.66′09′046—dc20   MN

ISBN 0–415–06815–0
ISBN 0–415–06816–9 (pbk.)

To my daughters Lucinda, Bryony and Anni – and to
Richard Middleton for his unfailing humour and support

Contents

Examples

Acknowledgements

I would like to thank many friends and colleagues for their encouragement whilst I was writing this book. I am particularly grateful to Richard Middleton for intellectual help; to Beth Humphries for her perceptive editing and to Jane Armstrong, Rebecca Barden and Moira Taylor of Routledge, who have been unfailingly supportive. I would also like to thank my parents, Ruth and Maurice, for their consistent support and encouragement. Above all, my thanks go to my children, Lucinda, Bryony and Anni for their invigorating mixture of love and inspiration. This book is dedicated to you.

Finally, I make grateful acknowledgement for permission to reprint the following song lyrics: to W/M William M. Roberts © Carlin Music Corp. for *Hey Joe* (Jimi Hendrix); to Westminster Music Ltd © Westminster Music Ltd of Suite 2.07, Plaza 535 Kings Road, London SW10 0SZ, international copyright secured, all rights reserved, for the following used by permission: *A Whiter Shade of Pale* (Gary Brooker/Keith Reid), *I Can Hear the Grass Grow* (Roy Wood), *See Emily Play* (Syd Barrett), *We Love You* (Mick Jagger/Keith Richard), *Astronomy Dominé* (Syd Barrett), *Midnight Rambler* (Mick Jagger/Keith Richard), *Satisfaction* (Mick Jagger/Keith Richard), *Sing This All Together* (Mick Jagger/Keith Richard), *Citadel* (Mick Jagger/Keith Richard), *Gomper* (Mick Jagger/Keith Richard), *In Another Land* (Bill Wyman), *2,000 Man* (Mick Jagger/Keith Richard), *She's A Rainbow* (Mick Jagger/Keith Richard), *2,000 Light Years From Home* (Mick Jagger/Keith Richard), *On With the Show* (Mick Jagger/Keith Richard), *Street Fighting Man* (Mick Jagger/Keith Richard), *Sympathy for the Devil* (Mick Jagger/Keith Richard); to Pink Floyd Music Publishers Limited © 1973 for *Speak to Me* (Mason), *Time* (Waters), *Money* (Waters), *Brain Damage* (Waters), *Breathe* (Waters/Gilmour/Wright), *The Great Gig in the Sky* (Wright), *Us and Them* (Waters/Wright,) *Eclipse* (Wright); to MCA Music Ltd © Northern Songs, all rights controlled and administered by MCA Music Ltd under licence from Northern Songs, for *Good Morning, Good Morning* (Lennon/McCartney), *All You Need is Love* (Lennon/McCartney), *With a Little Help From My*

Friends (Lennon/McCartney), *Lucy in the Sky with Diamonds* (Lennon/McCartney), *Getting Better* (Lennon/McCartney), *Fixing a Hole* (Lennon/McCartney), *She's Leaving Home* (Lennon/McCartney), *Being for the Benefit of Mr. Kite* (Lennon/McCartney), *Within You Without You* (Harrison), *When I'm Sixty-Four* (Lennon/McCartney), *Lovely Rita* (Lennon/McCartney), *Tomorrow Never Knows* (Lennon/McCartney), *A Day in the Life* (Lennon/McCartney), *Strawberry Fields Forever* (Lennon/McCartney), *Revolution* (Lennon/McCartney); to Donovan (Music) Ltd and Donovan Leitch for *You Just Gotta Know My Mind* (Leitch), *To Try for the Sun* (Leitch), *Sunshine Superman* (Leitch), *Mellow Yellow* (Leitch); to Warner Chappell Music Ltd for *I Feel Free* (Bruce/Brown), *Dance the Night Away (Bruce/Brown), Strange Brew* (Clapton/Collins/Pappalardi).

Every effort has been made to trace the appropriate copyright holders; where this has not been possible, those concerned should contact Routledge, London.

1 Introduction

Rock's superiority over previous popular musical forms is simply the result of its existence in a period of expanded and heightened social, political and psychological awareness, a period which made possible and necessary a hip and relevant popular music.[1]

Progressive rock and the counter-culture are often perceived as inseparable. Recognised as a social force, music was thought to say things of cultural and political significance, to have a message. Orientated towards a collective experience, rock appeared to provide the means whereby young people could explore the politics of consciousness, 'love, loneliness, depersonalisation, the search for the truth of the person and the attempt to set up an alternative life style'[2]. The question that arises is why there should have been this emphasis on a 'hip and relevant popular music'.

Was it, as Richard Neville wrote at the time, just symptomatic of an 'intense, spontaneous internationalism'?[3] 'From Berlin to Berkeley, from Zurich to Notting Hill, Movement members exchange a gut solidarity, sharing common aspirations, inspirations, strategy, style, mood and vocabulary. Long hair is their declaration of independence, pop music their esperanto and they puff pot in their peace pipe.'[4]

Roszak also draws attention to the international dimensions of the movement. 'Throughout the West (as well as in Japan and parts of Latin America), it is the young (qualified as perhaps only a minority of the university campus population) who find themselves cast as the only effective radical opposition within their societies.'[5]

Both Neville and Roszak, in common with most counter-cultural theorists, also discuss the divisions within the counter-cultural movement, the New Left, hippies and yippies. At the same time, Roszak points to the similarity of sensibility which united student and graduate activists and the drop-out hippies,

the continuum of thought and experience among the young which links together the new left sociology of Mills, the Freudian Marxism of Herbert Marcuse, the Gestalt-therapy anarchism of Paul Goodman, the

apocalyptic body mysticism of Norman Brown, the Zen-based psycho-
therapy of Alan Watts and finally Timothy Leary's impenetrably occult
narcissism, wherein the world and its woes may shrink at last to the size
of a mote in one's private psychedelic void.[6]

What is especially interesting is that contemporary analysts should draw
attention both to the divisions within the movement and to the broad
consistency in their antagonistic position towards the dominant culture. As
Roszak points out, 'What makes the youthful disaffiliation of our time a
cultural phenomenon rather than a political movement, is that it strikes
beyond ideology to the level of consciousness, seeking to transform our
deepest sense of the self, the environment.'[7]

It is, perhaps, this involvement with the self that has been particularly
relevant to the progressive rock musician in that it shifted the emphasis
away from the external constraints of the easily accessible, defined here as
known styles associated with particular bands, towards a more personalised
expression of musical exploration. With the recognition of musicians as
significant both to and within the counter-culture, who could not only voice
its concerns but also provoke reaction through their own musical and
personal confrontation with the mainstream culture, there was both a
support system and space to innovate. *Their Satanic Majesties Request* may
have appeared to move in a somewhat unlikely direction for a hard core r&b
band like the Rolling Stones, it may have been dubbed cynically a quick and
overall badly thought through response to the Beatles' *Sgt. Pepper* album,
but it reflected, nevertheless, the general trend towards a changed state of
musical consciousness. Musicians did not have to abandon a particular rock
style, but instead could add to it, select elements that continued to express
their own personal styles and incorporate techniques or spatial dimensions
which resonated with the new vocabulary of psychedelic rock[8] that had
come over from the West Coast of America.

Clearly this was not a new phenomenon; rock music is eclectic by nature.
What was new, however, was the emphasis on *meaning* in music which was
not simply tied to the lyrics, but spilled over into the sound itself. As Neville
wrote at the time: 'All the relevant sounds seemed somehow associated with
acid and universal love. The Beatles, Donovan, Cream, Jefferson Airplane,
Quicksilver Messenger Service, The Grateful Dead, The Doors, Country
Joe and the Fish all celebrated the acid experience and revived our faith in
each other.'[9]

This lumping together of so many diverse groups and the association of
acid and universal love with sounds in the music suggests that there was a
homology between musical and cultural characteristics. Progressive rock
was acknowledged as the major communicative organ of the counter-
culture. Its experimental nature mirrored concern for an alternative society.
Stylistic complexity, the elements of surprise, contradiction and uncertainty
suggested alternative meanings which supported the hippies' emphasis on

timeless mysticism. It appeared that the counter-culture and musical innovation were inseparable.

With progressive rock standing in a contradictory position to mainstream pop conventions, the question that arises is how it can be read as oppositional. How does progressive rock, from within its musical structures, articulate the socially mediated subjective experiences of the different groups within the counter-culture? Is it a simple contestation of existing musical frameworks, and how can a musical language express an alternative 'progressive' viewpoint? To what extent does this rely on personalised intuitional breaks, inflections and the breakdown of structure?

My initial analysis addresses the problem of the music itself – how it is arranged, instrumentation, style, and so on – but the question remains of how it provides social and cultural meanings. At one level it could be argued that music refers symbolically to such notions as physical space and movement. Musical shape and articulation are often accompanied by vocal and physical gestures. Pitch and timbre correlate with a sense of physical space and colour. Basic body rhythms (heartbeat, breathing) relate in turn to musical rhythms, while the tension/release patterning in melodic and rhythmic structures have associations with the pulse and breathing. Yet it is difficult to correlate these general connections with specific cultural contexts.

Progressive rock was located where particular sociological, cultural and musical developments crossed. It could therefore be argued that as the music was actually created in concrete cultural situations these orientated its received meaning in particular ways.[10] In reality, however, progressive rock was a particularly heterogeneous genre and while the variety of musical styles may have reflected the variety of radical movements and concerns within the counter-culture, the area of signification presents problems. In particular, the level of denotation seems lacking or, at best, unclear. Apart from some very clear references to the outside world (such as animal noises in the Beatles' *Good Morning*; clocks and alarms in Pink Floyd's *Dark Side of the Moon*), there is no system of objective reference to concepts and perceptions. On the other hand, it is possible to discuss connotations, since music was recognised as a symbolic act of self-liberation and self-realisation in which reality and musical experience were fused: the sound-shape, together with the socio-cultural element superimposed upon it, consolidate to form a distinct form of communication. At this point the diversity of musical styles within the genre of progressive rock becomes significant in establishing particular codes of behaviour through common musical codes.

For example, the counter-culture was largely concerned with alternative modes of living which involved, to a great extent, the use of drugs as a means of exploring the imagination and self-expression. Focused by a reading of Joel Fort's *The Pleasure Seekers: The Drug Crisis, Youth and Society*,[11] my analysis explores the way in which the different styles of progressive rock have common codes which convey a musical equivalent of hallucinogenic experience. These include the manipulation of timbres (blurred, bright, overlapping), upward movement (and its comparison with psychedelic flight), harmonies (lurching, oscillating), rhythms (regular, irregular), relationships (foreground, background) and collages which provide a point of comparison with more conventionalised, i.e. *normal* treatment.

Yet it is recognised that such associations quickly become conventionalised. As Middleton and Muncie point out,

> psychedelic elements in musical style are typically interpreted as such by reference to a sub-culture of drug usage; in other words, they are defined in this way primarily because hippies said they should be. A whole group of connotations, arising from our knowledge of the drug culture, then settles on the music. But this culture has already been defined in this way partially because of the existence in it of this particular kind of music. The meaning of drug usage is affected by the meaning of the associated music . . . The system is perfectly structured internally . . . but has no necessary *purchase* on it from without.[12]

While my consideration of the music has been influenced to some extent by this awareness of intra-cultural interpretations, I have tried to establish the meaning of psychedelic elements through an examination of the musical codes involved and, more important, their interrelationship. This has also made possible an identification of whether or not a group has simply 'lifted' the more general psychedelic musical codes (e.g. blurred overlapping timbres, bright tinkly sounds) in an attempt to capitalise on the popularity of acid rock.

Although the initial analysis at first focuses on the music of Cream, Jimi Hendrix and Pink Floyd, who were considered by contemporary commentators to be influential progressive rock musicians and of interest to the counter-culture, it is apparent that the counter-culture was by no means their total audience. Similarly, while the Beatles' *Sgt. Pepper* album was considered especially influential in setting the agenda for the counter-culture in Britain, and in particular in focusing attention on hallucinogenics, its general popularity points to the conclusion that even in the presence of a sharply delineated relationship between progressive rock and the counter-culture, musical styles are rarely the exclusive property of one specific group. This point was borne out in my analysis of 1967 chart singles which dealt with psychedelic experience, and Pink Floyd's *Dark Side of the Moon*, which topped the LP charts for three years from 1972 to 1974. Conversely, while the Rolling Stones' role as anti-establishment musicians reverberated with the counter-culture's stand against mainstream society, there is little to suggest that the group specifically identified with counter-cultural ideology. This is equally true of Hendrix, whose refusal to be associated with the Black Panther party is well documented.

So there is little to suggest that progressive rock was the exclusive

property of the counter-culture. Rather, it seems that there were correspon-
dences between musical practices and social relationships and the way in
which these were lived out at the level of cultural symbols. Progressive rock,
like all music, relied on communication and positive identification. As such,
it had an intrinsically collective character which suggested that it was
capable of transmitting the affective identities, attitudes and behavioural
patterns of the group(s) identifying with it.

Finally, while it is recognised that progressive rock (in common with
other popular forms of music) is primarily an aural experience, that it is
performed, stored and distributed in a non-written form and that musical
notation is not, therefore, the only key to analysis, I have nevertheless found
it helpful to use manuscript as a graphic way of leading the reader through
selected areas of the text. In particular, my analysis of psychedelic coding in
Jimi Hendrix relates musical notation to hallucinogenic experience and as
such should be read in context. Clearly, it could not be assumed that the use
of a particular chord sequence, for example, always carries with it the same
connotations.

2   Cream, Hendrix and Pink Floyd

Commentaries on 'progressive rock' are generally framed in terms of *becoming*. 'Rock became progressive',[1] 'Underground music' became 'progressive music'.[2] The mid-sixties letters page of *Melody Maker* highlights the 'emergence' of rock in which *progress* is measured in terms of musical ideas and techniques: 'Hendrix: Progressive and beautiful in his ideas'; 'Clapton: Progressing with ideas and techniques'.[3] Musicians such as Cream, Pink Floyd, Hendrix and the Beatles are credited with liberating rock from pop[4] in terms of qualities of 'art' and 'genius'. Equally there is a focus on 'relevant sounds' which, in the summer of 1967, were tied to the psychedelic,[5] thus raising the question of whether rock, acid rock and progressive rock are interchangeable terms.

Middleton and Muncie's observation that 'progressive rock (which we can take roughly as the music of the counter-culture) is a particularly heterogenous genre'[6] also points to the problem of categorisation, of whether it is possible to arrive at a definition which can satisfactorily describe its range of musical styles. Definition is further problematised by the importance attributed to rock by the counter-culture itself: 'it was thought to say things of cultural and political significance, to have a message'.[7] This would suggest that there is a relationship between the musical form and its cultural use with the implication that the *meaning* of progressive rock cannot fully be understood without a consideration of extra-musical factors.

During the late sixties, three groups considered to be of particular significance in the development of British progressive rock were Cream, the Jimi Hendrix Experience and Pink Floyd, all formed in 1965–66. As they were just as influential in the development of psychedelic rock their music will also be analysed for psychedelic coding to determine the extent to which acid rock and progressive rock are comparable terms.

Cream was formed by Eric Clapton (guitar), Ginger Baker (drums) and Jack Bruce (bass and most of the vocals). Baker and Bruce were originally in the Graham Bond Organisation, a group whose virtuoso jazz and blues format was inherited by Cream when they recruited Eric Clapton from John Mayall's Bluesbreakers, a group famous for their accurate recreation of the sound and style of such contemporary Chicago blues players as Buddy Guy,

Otis Rush and Magic Sam.[8] According to Clapton, Cream was originally planned as a blues trio which 'aimed to extend the expressive potential and aesthetic quality of blues-based rock music',[9] through an emphasis on improvisational technique based on individual virtuosity.

Cream's pedigree was impeccable and any doubts about the three musicians' ability to play as a group were initially dispelled after their début appearance at the 1966 Windsor Festival and the release of their first album, *Fresh Cream*. The group's second UK single success, *I Feel Free*, entered the charts in January 1967, moving up to No. 12 in February. Written by Jack Bruce and Pete Brown, *I Feel Free*[10] draws heavily on the blues tradition in the basic falling shape of the vocal, the strong use of repetitive phrases and short motifs and the declamatory vocal style of the chorus. The song is based on two contrasting styles: the first gentle and floating around the beat, the second more didactic with a strong emphasis on the vocal and the walking bass line. A sense both of freedom and of continuity is achieved by the subtle interplay of the basic motifs established in the introduction.

Preceded by an electronically distanced guitar chord, the opening riff of *I Feel Free* immediately establishes a sensitive interplay between the three musicians. The 'bom bom bom ba bom bom' of the vocal riff is neatly dissected by clapping on the second and fourth beat before the vocal entry 'I feel free' on the third beat of the third bar with the hummed 'ah' adding a feeling of fluid movement which feeds the meaning of the title 'I Feel Free'.

The two verses, while based on the same harmonies as the opening riff – (E–E/D), feature a new rhythmic ostinato. The double-tracked vocal picks up on the original hummed melody line, following the inflection of the words with accents between beats as well as on them to continue the aural sensation of fluid movement generated in the opening riff. The effect is of rhythmic subtlety as each player expands on the small motifs. The use of the two-chord harmonic unit works towards a continuous sense of motion which is accentuated by the overlaying of the off-the-beat guitar riff against the rhythm of the vocal. Yet a feeling of continuity is created as the verses expand on the opening riff and the concept of freedom is opened up both musically and lyrically.

The harmonic structure beneath the verses is simple and concise. The six four-bar phrases are based on E–E/D and this constant repetition moves against any sensation of completion. The mood generated is one of a gently floating high,[11] which is complemented by the feeling of unfettered space suggested by the lyrics:

> You, you're all I want to know
> I feel free. . .

The chorus again makes use of the same harmonies, thus establishing both a sense of continuity and a common structural framework capable of infinite variation. This time, for example, the mood is far more positive, with the walking bass line punctuating the vocal as it moves towards a dramatic assertion of personal freedom.

Initially, the heavily repetitive structure of the song suggests an unchanging 'present': there are no developments, only variations. At the same time, the simple harmonic structure works towards the freeing of melody and form and Clapton's solo in particular, with its long single notes on the one hand and flurries of quick notes on the other, the use of bent notes and sensuous vibrato (known as the 'woman tone') take on a new significance as they float around the beat, also suggesting individualistic freedom.[12] While this could be read simply as a solo break which demonstrates an intimate, physical feeling for sound, 'in music a specific unit or parameter usually signifies very generally; its precise meaning is only fixed when it's considered in relation to other units and parameters within a total structure'.[13] In *I Feel Free* Clapton's solo break is contextualised by the chorus with its strongly declamatory stress on personal freedom. Initially the harmonic structure remains the same as in the verse although the rhythm is more assertive and on the beat. There is an emphasis on changed perceptions:

I can walk down the street
There's no one there
Though the pavements are one huge crowd

This suggests hallucinogenic experience. Psychedelic experience can involve 'changes in time (and other sensory perception); diminished inhibitions and symbolic overtones, heightened sensations'.[14] Musically psychedelic coding focuses on *alternative meanings* and involves a correlation of drug experience and stylistic characteristics.[15]

After the break, the chorus returns, and the more adventurous chord structure and vocal line move towards a sense of climax. Within the context of the song there is the suggestion of an hallucinatory high and as the final verse enters, there is an aural sensation of floating around the beat. As such there is a implicit association with an acid experience whereby words and phrases can take on an unreal significance to become totally absorbing within a changed state of consciousness. The gentle floating around the beat suggests a state of 'tripping','orbiting', where the fixed point (E–E/D) can take on a new reality. This is reinforced by the hallucinatory condition described by the lyrics and the way in which the vocal follows the irregular accenting of the words (with accents between beats as well as on them):

Dance floor is like the sea
Ceiling is the sky

The electronic distancing of the voice on the repeated 'I feel free' also pulls on the physical experience of LSD whereby speech and images are often blurred. Finally the coda reinforces the feeling of floating around the beat and its lack of finality in the gradual fade-out is reassuring: the experience can be repeated.

While press reviews focused on the length of Clapton's solos, Cream emphasised the importance of absorbing different musical styles and then coming up with original ideas. Their trip to America in February 1967 provided an opportunity to meet the Mothers of Invention; Frank Zappa, whose combination of sharp wit and respect for musical form and discipline greatly appealed to Clapton. At the same time, the band experienced at first hand LSD as an integral part of American underground philosophy and *Disraeli Gears* was released after 'an acid summer . . . in the company of George Harrison and John Lennon, both heavily into LSD'.[16]

Clapton brought a whole range of guitar innovations to bear in *Disraeli Gears*. Overall the effects were an amalgam of heavy blues guitar and Hendrix-inspired effects, in particular the wah-wah pedal, fuzz tone and reverb. *SWLABR* (*She Walks Like a Bearded Rainbow*) was another Bruce/Brown number with a fuzz-tone solo. The song is based predominantly on a simple harmonic structure C–F and again relies heavily on repetitive structures. The three verses are underpinned by a riff which supports a falling vocal line with the chorus heightening the tension through Bruce's preacher-like delivery and blues intonation of:

Coming to me with that soulful look on your face
Coming like you've never done one wrong thing. . . .

The blurred timbres of Clapton's solo then lead directly to the psychedelically charged third verse. Here the conjunction of the electronically manipulated timbres with the associations of 'fantastic colours', 'such good responses' pull on the associations of a good trip, with the problems established in the first two verses ('coming to me in the morning, leaving me at night', 'returning to me a-cryin', when he throws you out') being resolved through psychedelic release.

Yet there remains a sense of uncertainty. While the 'pure feel', 'good responses' connote a feeling of positive release, the final 'but the rainbow has a beard', along with the falling shape of the guitar riff with its blue notes, suggests a possible unresolved tension. There is a suggestion that acid, 'that rainbow feel', 'that pure feel' may not resolve the traditional blues problem of 'woman trouble' established in the first two verses.

Dance the Night Away is again based on heavily repetitive structures. The verses fall into two sections. The first section is built over a bass riff with the vocal line rising and falling with the inflection of the words:

Gonna build myself a castle
High up in the clouds

In the second section the bass moves to a steady crotchet beat, with the lead guitar supporting the vocal ('Lose those streets and crowds, dance the night away') with electronically distorted, twanging chords.

The lyrics suggest hallucinogenic experience and in conjunction with the double-tracked rising and falling shape of the vocal line and the driving pace of the riff move towards a musical equivalent of an exhilarated high. The song also reads like a tribute to the Byrds, with Clapton playing a mandolinesque 12-string guitar reminiscent of Roger McGuinn.

Cream continued to work through the winter of 1967, including a TV spectacular in Holland, and in February 1968 they had a second tour of America, 'five and a half months of one-nighters – no British band ever embarked on such a colossal touring programme before, nor earned so much money'.[17] However, as Clapton pointed out,

> Everybody was getting their rocks off too much, somehow, and it was just burning up very quickly. Everyone got into too much of a heavy ego-trip. Virtuosos and all that kind of rubbish. The group started out as one thing and turned into something else. We really thought we were the kings of our instruments. No-one else could come near what we were doing. And it was all through the adulation we were being given. The audience was to blame as much as anyone else. Because they pushed us to those heights. You should never allow yourself to think at any time that you're the best at what you're doing – it's ridiculous. But we definitely did think that – every one of us![18]

By July it was confirmed that Cream were splitting up and a double album, *Wheels of Fire*, was released which was recorded half in the studio and half live. In many ways the record was similar to the Beatles' double *White Album*, an aggregate of individual effort rather than a rounded and fully integrated co-operative album, and again Bruce/Brown songs dominate. Significantly Clapton contributed no material, leaving all the lead vocals on the studio album to Bruce and taking the lead on only two numbers, both blues standards, *Born Under a Bad Sign* and *Sitting on Top of the World*.

Those Were the Days brings to the fore Baker's influence, which is reflected not only in the insistent yet elusive drum rhythms but also in the complex and subtle rhythmic interplay of the three musicians. The mood of the song is established by Jack Bruce, who introduces the *Those Were the Days* motif, and is built on two contrasting styles: a fast-moving four-bar phrase which is supported by a heavily accented riff taken from bars five and six of the introduction and an instrumental section. This is initiated by Bruce's vocal 'Those were the days' which picks up on the bass riff of bars one and two of the introduction, this time transposed up a fifth. Subtle changes in rhythm are effected by stretching the crotchet of the first bar to a minim and extending the notes of the second bar to semibreves. The vocal D–C on 'days' is supported by D major–C major chords which are repeated twice before moving downwards to Em. Over the top chimes anticipate the words of the next vocal entry, 'Golden cymbals flying on ocarina sounds'.

The chorus is also based on the 'Those Were the Days' motif, which becomes the basis for simple repetition and variation. The singing is light, almost falsetto, the echoing 'yes they were' is sung in thirds, and with the use of repetition and the nostalgic 'those were the days' over the final A minor harmonies, moves towards a sentimentality more often associated with pop songs.

The last verse, however, suggests that the nostalgia may have psychedelic connotations. Preceded by Clapton's guitar break which starts on a top Bb, the solo focuses on configurations of vibrant bent-up notes and sliding glissandos to effect a sense of 'tripping' around the underlying beat. The lyrics then pick up on these connotations by focusing on perceptual changes which appear to reflect psychedelic experience. 'Ordinary boundaries and controls between the self and the environment and within the self are loosened':[19]

> Tie your painted shoes and dance,
> Blue daylight in your hair

Deserted Cities of the Heart reflects again the intimate musical relationship between Baker, Bruce and Clapton. The most striking effect of the song is its pace and drive. The bass guitar riff of the verse is strongly rhythmic and pushes towards the beat. Baker, meanwhile, drums relentlessly and minutely against Bruce's off-beat singing. The rhythm guitar is strummed initially in crotchet beats, but as the song continues, the rhythmic composition of each verse varies in detail, so that its effect is almost kaleidoscopic.

Certain rhythmic effects continue throughout the composition. The eight-bar verse is built over the bass riff, although this is modified in bars three and seven when the song changes from ¢ to ¾. Melodically, verses one and two are identical. The vocal is narrow-ranged and based on a nagging motif which creates a subtle opposition between the predominantly D major harmonies and the flattened C in the melody. Verse three is based on the same riff and harmonic structure but this time the flattened C is more pronounced to cause an increasing sense of tension.

In verse four, again based on the same underlying structure, the feeling of tension is heightened by starting the vocal line on a high repeated D and by changing the second and fourth bars, which rise dramatically to F♮. In conjunction with the words: 'the sun is black' and 'it's cold inside' and contextualised by 'on this dark street' and the focus on darkness and death, the blue notes impart a plaintive pessimism reminiscent of the blues.[20]

All four choruses are based on the alternation of voice and guitar/drum beat and, like the verse, the vocal is characterised by off-beat phrasing which follows the irregular accents of the words, with accents between beats as well as on them.

The harmonic and melodic resources in *Deserted Cities of the Heart* are limited. The melodic line of the verse is motivic and in verses one and two never exceeds the interval of a fifth. The use of a repeated note (A occurs twenty-four times out of a possible thirty-two in the verse; D, fourteen times out of twenty-one in the chorus) against a basic riff has a cumulative effect which underpins the meaning of the words, the realisation that time has run out and that one is locked into a bleak and unchanging present.

At the same time, the musical effect of the simple harmonic structures, the riff of the verse, the scale-wise descent of the bass in the chorus, is to free the melody and form and the interplay of the three musicians throughout the song is subtle. Phrases are built up out of repetitions and variations of the small motifs to create an intimacy of musical sound and gesture. This is at its strongest during Clapton's solo. Throughout the break the texture is clearly differentiated; each line is precise and fits tightly against the others. The solo line itself is played with tremendous precision. Razor-sharp licks are coupled with elegant loops and swirls to create a miasmic sound which contrasts with the underlying rumble of Bruce's bass with its tonal inflections on the drone-like D. This gives the break a heavy rock feeling. The bass drum is also unusual as the tom-toms which occur both before and after the bars analysed are absent in this section. Despite the use of synthesiser there is little sense of electronic experimentation. Instead the solo relies on Clapton's actual handling of the guitar and the fluid emotionalism of his playing, which, blues-like, builds on the original vocal line figures (see Example 1).

While *Deserted Cities of the Heart* can again be read as formulaic in that it depends on repetitive structures and a blues scale (based on D) there is little doubt that Cream extended the expressive potential of blues-based music. The interplay of the three musicians in the break, for example, exhibits both a sensitive awareness of the others' musical line, while emphasising the individualistic potential of each instrument through a physical feeling for sound and musical gesture. Baker plays basically on the beat, but reverses the usual order of the hi-hat and ride cymbal beats and omits the tom-tom to effect a heavy-rock sound. This complements the metallic vibrancy of Clapton's solo, which has now dispensed with the woman tone which characterised his earlier performance. At the same time, the solo continues to exhibit the basic characteristic of Clapton's blues-based style in its vibrant tone and the speech-like phrasing – the extended phrasing in bars 4–6 contrasting with the more punchy, declamatory style of bars 7–9, the subtle rhythmic inflections of bar 10. Bruce's bass guitar is equally subtle in effect. The inflections on the drone-like D are given an added intensity by the overlay of notes on bars 3–6 and 9–10 and these too suggest improvisation in the changing phrase shapes as well as an underlying feeling for binary oppositions in the tug between the C♮/C♯ of the blue scale.

As the foregoing analyses show, Cream's musical style was strongly influenced by the blues. This comes through particularly in the heavily repetitive structuring of the riffs, the repetition of phrases and short motifs and the use of blues scales, the falling shapes of the vocal and the use of call and response between vocal and guitar. Clapton's guitar style is equally influenced by the blues, in particular the ringing guitar tone of B.B. King. The underlying mood of each song is equally critical to the use made of blues resources. Out of context, the repetitive structures could read like formulaic clichés (for example, there is often an alternation between a syncopated bass riff and a descending chromatic scale), but when allied to Baker's constantly varying drum rhythms and the nuances in Clapton's lead guitar, the effect is one of subtle interplay. This is at its most marked during the improvisatory passages, for example in *Deserted Cities of the Heart* where all three musicians respond to the inflections in Clapton's solo. There is a development of the expressive potential of the blues which often feeds psychedelic coding. *SWLABR* (*She Walks Like a Bearded Rainbow*), for example, focuses hallucinogenic escape while encoding an underlying unresolved tension.

Overall, then, there is both exploitation and development of the blues. The sense of progression relies in the main on the musicianship of Clapton, Bruce and Baker and their ability to compose and perform music which draws on their own background in the blues yet is sufficiently open in structure to allow for individualised improvisation and corporate interplay. Blues resources are evident throughout, but at the same time there is space

Example 1 Deserted Cities of the Heart

Example 1 cont.

for innovation, eg the incorporation of psychedelic coding, fuzz tone, wah-wah pedal and reverb in Clapton's guitar playing, blues/jazz, blues/classical, blues/Indian fusions, the overlay of different styles of melody lines and lyrics which relate to contemporary themes. Cream's virtuosity goes beyond the extended instrumental improvisations which were the main focus of reviews. These provided the most dramatic evidence of the virtuoso techniques of the individual musicians, but it could equally be argued that the vocal and textural strength of the band was equally significant in developing the expressive potential of a blues-based rock music.

Cream's influence on rock extended up to the mid-1970s with heavy-metal bands. As John Pidgeon points out, they were 'the first band to find major success *because* of their musicianship, rather than in spite of it'.[21] However limited their repertoire (and Cream wrote only twenty-seven songs over the band's three years), their musicality and technical skill was indisputable and they gave the blues movement a much needed springboard. Numerous bands emerged during 1967 and 1968 – Fleetwood Mac, Free, Jethro Tull and the Jeff Beck Group – but it is generally acknowledged that along with Cream, Jimi Hendrix can be credited with establishing virtuosity as a major parameter in blues-based rock music.

Hendrix was one of Clapton's most devoted admirers. He had first met Cream in 1966 and acknowledged them as the inspiration behind his own three-piece band, the Jimi Hendrix Experience. The Jimi Hendrix Experience first supported Cream at the London Polytechnic but

> prior to that, Chas Chandler had brought Hendrix to a London Club where Cream was playing and he jammed with them: for Clapton, the experience was a revelation. 'My God, I couldn't believe it! It really blew my mind. Totally.' After that, Clapton, usually in the company of Pete Townshend, saw every Hendrix jam session in London during 1966, bar two.[22]

By 1966 both Clapton and Townshend had been acclaimed as virtuoso performers in the fields of lyrical and rhythmic guitar playing respectively and as Clapton pointed out, to find someone who could do both with such staggering virtuosity and presence was a pleasant surprise.

Prior to his move to London, Hendrix's musical career had included package tours with Solomon Burke and Wilson Pickett. His strongest influence came from the serious blues guitarists of the American South – Muddy Waters, Willie Dixon and Little Walter – and on one occasion he backed his idol, B.B. King. Other temporary engagements included backing Little Richard, Jackie Wilson, Wilson Pickett and Curtis Knight and for a time he played with the Isley Brothers, the first band to give him a chance to play lead guitar. This broad-based experience in the clubs made him equally conversant with jazz, saxophone swing, rhythm and blues, gospel and soul.

Chas Chandler, former bass player of the Animals and now a rock manager, saw Hendrix playing at the Cafe Wha in Greenwich Village in

1966 and brought him back to London where they auditioned a rhythm section which resulted in the engagement of Noel Redding (bass) and Mitch Mitchell (drums). Calling the band the Jimi Hendrix Experience, they played their first public engagement at Paris Olympia.

Hey Joe, with flip side *Stone Free* was the group's first single, and was released on December 16, 1966. By this time Hendrix had spent four months playing the London clubs: the Marquee, the Upper Cut, the Bag-O-Nails and the short lived 7½ Club. A review in *Melody Maker*, 'Caught in the Act' focused on his powerful psychedelic blues style, but the press generally wrote him off as so much loud, useless noise, calling him 'The Wild Man from Borneo' or 'The Crazy Black Man'. Rather than fight the image the group encouraged it, hoping it would increase their following in the underground. *Hey Joe* musically reinforced this image.

> Mysterious, menacing, and dynamically very well paced, the record in effect picked up on the blues where the Rolling Stones had left the idiom after topping the British charts with *Little Red Rooster* in 1964, and *Hey Joe* ... made the British top ten early in 1967. Just as Britain was beginning to feel the reverberations of the drug culture of San Francisco, here was a young black man from the West Coast with frizzy hair, outrageously colourful clothes, and no inhibitions about using the guitar as a sexual symbol.[23]

But as Mike Clifford points out, 'Hendrix had everything going for him – he had a supremely cool vocal drawl, dope-and-Dylan oriented lyrics, the acid dandyism of his clothes and the stirring element of black sexual fantasy.'[24]

Hey Joe is based on a simple repetitive harmonic structure with the introduction establishing the inherent menacing mood of the song with a moody, blues-like riff. The vocal is based on a heavily repetitive falling motif, coloured by inflection and muttered comments :

> 'Hey Joe, where you goin' with that gun in your hand
> (I said)
> Hey Joe, where you goin' with that gun in your hand'

After a shouted 'I gave her the gun. I shot her. Yes, I did. I took the gun and I shot her' the second verse leads into Hendrix's guitar solo. This is based on scale figures which move around the principal chord structure: three bars on G major, two bars on E minor. The effect of the harmonies is to free the melody line (the structure is easily extended to create breaks of an irregular length) while the form itself isn't constrained by a set harmonic sequence (such as the 12-bar blues). The progressions also provide harmonic motion under the strongly rhythmic figures which are themselves punctuated by Hendrix comments, 'Shoot her one more time baby' (see Example 2).

Hendrix had first heard *Hey Joe* when jamming with Arthur Lee of Love, but whereas Lee relied on a mixture of muttered vocals and a guitar line borrowed from Jackie De Shannon's *When You Walk In The Room*,

Example 2 Hey Joe

Hendrix shows more the influence of two of his guitar heroes, John Lee Hooker and Albert King. The introduction, for example, with its accented G, the underpinning in the vocal line with the long decay on the D over which Hendrix mutters 'I said' reflects the moody and menacing style of Hooker, while the casual dexterity in the lead break is reminiscent more of Albert King. The influence of B.B. King is also present in the sensuous articulation in the break, the flurries of quick notes contrasting with the sustained G and glissando fall in bar 7. The basic falling pattern which was established in the vocal is also there, and is a typical r&b formula. However, as Hendrix himself once replied to an interviewer who was comparing his style with Clapton, 'but like, the blues is what we're supposed to dig. . . . Sometimes the notes might sound like it, but it's a different scene between those notes'.[25] Thus, while there are blue notes, pitch inflection, 'vocalised' guitar tone, triplet beats and off-beat accenting and a call and response relationship in Hendrix's own commentary to his guitar solo and verse line, the way in which these elements are pulled together are typically Hendrix. The sustain tone, which originated with B.B. King, takes on an even more overt sexuality, which was particularly evident in live performance when Hendrix would play the guitar with his teeth or with strongly masturbatory connotations to feed both the rhythmic emphasis of the guitar line and the words themselves: 'I caught her messin' with another man'.[26]

In January 1967 Nick Jones' article 'Hendrix – On the crest of a Fave Rave' provided a formative account of the basic ingredients for progressive rock: 'The Hendrix sound is what England hasn't yet evolved – but desperately needs. It's a weaving, kaleidoscope of tremor and vibration, discords and progressions.'[27]

Hey Joe, was issued on the Polydor label and was followed up by an appearance on the penultimate edition of the British TV series 'Ready, Steady Go'. This was followed by *Purple Haze* and the début album *Are You Experienced?* (September 1967).

Purple Haze, named after a particular brand of acid, is overtly concerned with LSD experience and effect:

Purple Haze was in my brain
Lately things they don't seem the same

Example 3 Purple Haze

The energy, use of distortion, fuzz,[28] wah wah and loudness coupled with precise and sinuous scalic riffs are comparable to *Hey Joe*, but this time the sexual focus, the betrayal of the male by the female and the violent consequences are shifted to give a sense of timelessness: 'Don't know if I'm coming up or down'. *Purple Haze* begins with a bass pedal E under A# on bass and lead guitar, the two bars creating an underlying beat which works to establish a bonding between performer and audience.[29] The pulse-like beat continues in the next two bars, but here the A# disappears as Hendrix moves into the opening riff with its characteristic bending up of notes and dipping vibratos. Whilst this is basically a pentatonic blues riff, the extremes of distortion blur the actual pitching of the notes and the discordant partials make it practically impossible to hear the pitch. However, given the blues logic of Hendrix's other songs it is probable that the underlying structure is based on the chords of E–G–A which support the earlier vocal line (see Example 3).

The riff has the typical feeling of muscle and crunch common to most Hendrix numbers, and this comes through particularly in the tonal quality created by the electronic distortion, the fuzz and the resultant discordant partials. The expectations generated in the opening riff are also picked up in the main break which moves towards an overt theatricality with its hammered and pulled-off notes, the jittered bursts of broken words over the free-flowing improvisation with its wild yet controlled sense of energy. The

Example 4 Purple Haze

logic of the melodic shape of the line, the downward curve from C# to B subtly supports the more overt frenzy of the delivery itself (see Example 4).

Throughout the entire solo the impression is of doubling at the octave above, a possible effect of electronic distortion or alternatively some sort of partial harmonic. In some bars the lower octave predominates, in others the upper, with the clearest 'shifts' to the higher octave occurring at bars 2 and 8.

As an acid track, the torn sounds and muttered syllables work within the overall shape of the lead guitar line which moves from top C# to B. (example 5a). The movement into the 'trip' is accompanied by upward moving figures (example 5b), the drums gradually moving from a highly active and syncopated rhythm into a fast but even pulse in quavers (example 5c). In the lead break, high notes, sliding amplifications and the sheer volume of noise move against the continuous arterial throb of the rhythm to juxtapose two realities – the throb of the continuous bass heartbeat against the exhilarated high of Hendrix's guitar solo, which is intensified by the doubling at the octave effect (see Examples 5a–c).

For the listener, the sheer volume of noise works towards the drowning of personal consciousness. The simultaneous underlying pulsating rhythm and the heightened sensation of raw power rip through the distorted amplification of the guitar sound with its sinuous *tripping* around the basic notes. The melody line is simple and based on a recurring motif which moves towards an incantatory, mesmeric effect. Again there is an indication that the song reflects the state of mind on a hallucinogenic trip. When the passage is played at half-speed on a tape recorder, the word 'haze' in particular vibrates, dips and moves upwards to suggest a sense of fixation, and this effect is also present on 'funny' and 'sky', where the dip shapes create a strong feeling of floating around the beat.

Overall, the use of repetition in the song works towards a mood of obsessiveness and absorption. This is reflected in the motif which constitutes the total melodic structure of the vocal line, and while there are minor variations based on inflection which bend with the words, its constant use moves ultimately towards fixation and total absorption within the 'purple haze'. The final vocal phrase, for example, with its strong dip shapes and muttered comments, is supported by a pulsating beat which stops suddenly as Hendrix mutters 'help me, help me, help me'. The effect is that of loss of time, the underlying beat has gone and all that remains is the distanced voice and a sense of other-worldliness. The total effect of *Purple Haze* is one of drifting and while the lead break is fairly metrical with most of the bars being in eighths or sixteenths plus ornaments, the occasional deflection of accents from weak to strong beats creates a feeling of being within a different time scale.

This sensation of drifting is also fed by phrasing and articulation. In the lead break the guitar meanders in an almost raga-like noodling around the notes, again suggestive of a state of tripping where a fixed idea/concept/

Example 5 (a, b, c) Purple Haze

point takes on a new reality. In conjunction with the feedback and distortion there is a feeling of incoherence. The high registers are almost pure noise and resonate with the imagery of the words: 'You've got me blowing, blowing my mind'.

While *Purple Haze* makes use of many blues features, an overall anti-structure comes through in the aural experience of the delivery, the dense sound, the distorted slide notes, the muttered, broken questions:

Help me, help me

the deep-throated answer:

Purple haze, Purple haze
You go on and on till the end of time
oooh noo, oooh noo. . .

and the final rising crescendo of the high-pitched E vibrato.

Hendrix's extreme use of a fuzz effect whereby even the slightest touch of the guitar gives off a full-volumed sound also feeds the underlying sense of disorganisation.

Other effects used in *Purple Haze* are the wah-wah pedal, reverb, echo, phase and tremolo, all of which are common today but were relatively new at the time. Although not used as extensively as fuzz, they allowed Hendrix to extend the expressive potential of the blues; in conjunction with the psychedelic connotations of the words, the song moves towards a theatrical enactment of a drug-induced state.

Love or Confusion has an equally simple harmonic structure and is based on the chords of G–G6–F–F6. The effect is to free the vocal line, which follows the natural inflection of the words with accents both on and off the beat.

Is that the stars in the sky
Or is it raining far from now

The rising and falling phrase shapes and the muttered asides support the underlying meaning of the words, rising on the word 'love', sinking on 'confusion'. This confusion is intensified by Hendrix's guitar playing, which appears to be superimposed on the vocal. It is neither in dialogue with the voice, nor does it fill in gaps as in the blues, but instead provides its own vocal line. The effect is of two simultaneous melodies, both in the G minor pentatonic blues scale. The chromaticism in the bass line provides a certain 'dizziness' which again feeds the idea of confusion (see Example 6).

The effect of the passage is of noise, generated in the main by Hendrix's use of fuzz tone which sounds at times almost like snare drum accents. This functions to articulate the beginning or end of a section and here the fuzz together with the low grinding sound of the bass guitar move against the rests and the drum roll. At the same time, the other instruments come briefly into focus, doubling the bass line to create a moment of coherence. The rhythm guitar actually doubles the snare drum part, but since it is so sustained and relatively free of high frequencies, the sounds are distinct. The vocal line bends heavily, with the muttered 'or is it confusion' acting almost as commentary on the sounds of the passage.

The words are strongly psychedelic in their associations of colour and confusion:

Oh, my head is pounding, pounding,
going 'round and 'round and 'round and 'round
Must there always be these colours?

With the acute distortions of fuzz sound and the tripping around notes in the lead break, the words move towards a sensation of movement through time and space. The endless feedback and distortion move the listener into an equivalent state of incoherence, the montage of sound effects, reverb, echo, tremolo and fuzz, resonating with the vocal message 'pounding, pounding, going 'round and 'round and 'round and 'round'.

Hendrix' lead break with its bent-up notes and glissandi equally suggests flight. It is here that the psychedelic fuses with space rock: the electronically distorted notes encode the unpredictability of hallucinogenic search, the lack of certainty of a good/bad trip, with the unknown element in space travel. Hendrix's exploration of space reads like a negative reaction to the mainstream rather than a positive move towards engaging in cultural quest.[30] The use of distortion and fuzz creates an unknown element which can suggest uncertainty. This also comes through in the way in which Hendrix tuned his guitar. The top string was often tuned to D or Eb and the excessive bending and use of the wah-wah pedal served to obscure the actual notes played.

Example 6 Love or Confusion

Example 6 Love or Confusion – cont.

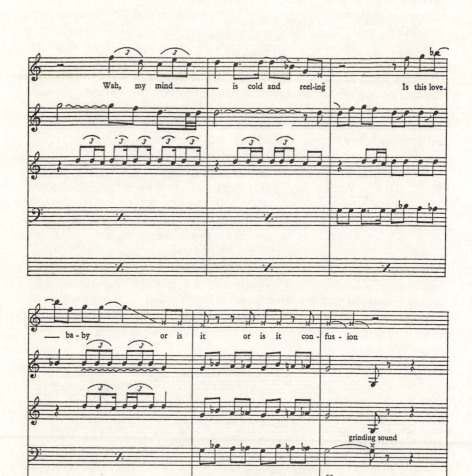

The extreme use of noise, in conjunction with the hypnotic nature of the Hendrix sound with its overwhelming energy and drive, created a means through which he could tune into the 'collective unconscious' of his audience. This provoked the mass sexual ecstasy often associated with his concerts, which moved towards a corporeal sense of tribal unity. At this point, Hendrix's personal expansion of human consciousness would fuse with the collective experience of the hallucinogenic in the exploration of the self through mind-expanding drugs: 'Will it burn me if I touch the sun, so big, so round?'.

Along with the overpowering energy of his guitar playing, allied to unusual sound effects (running his hand up and down the fretboard, banging the guitar and feeding these sounds through fuzz) there is the implication of a new language of sound which equates with the hallucinogenic space exploration implicit in the lyrics.

> Mild physical sensations, particularly in the limbs, occur, but the main dimensions . . . are perceptual . . . primarily visual, but also [including] the other individual sensory modalities and sometimes a blending or synesthesia so that one 'hears' something seen, or 'tastes' something touched. With the eyes closed, kaleidoscopic colors and a wide array of geometric shapes and specific objects . . . are often seen . . . . Illusions can occur and sometimes, depending on the interaction of the many important human and drug variables, hallucinations.[31]

While *Love or Confusion* continues to draw on blues resources especially in the single-note attack with long decay and glissando fall, the basic melodic falling pattern, eg 'Is this love, baby, or is it confusion' – is equally typical of r&b. The forcefulness in Hendrix's guitar style can be traced back to his early experience in r&b and rock 'n' roll, but generally structures and style are growth points rather than working barriers. The improvisations and the often incoherent instrumental melody/sound, the apparently disordered, random and electronically dominated noise, the never-ending effect of the reverb create a kaleidoscopic effect. Layers of sound appear to grow out of one another in a continuous flow to provide a musical metaphor for the endlessness of space. The emphasis on noise and the chaotic sound of Hendrix's playing also support the idea of confusion:

> Oh, my head is pounding, pounding,
> Going 'round and 'round and 'round

The effect is anarchic, a move against reality (with its emphasis on logic) and as such there is a fusion with the psychedelic, the unpredictability of hallucinogenic search, the juxtaposition of unknown colours with chaos.

Hey Joe, Purple Haze, The Wind Cries Mary and *Love or Confusion* were constantly performed by Hendrix in concert and appeared on seven of his LPs including the live recording *Woodstock*. They appear to be representative not only of his particular style of performance, but also of his focus on the psychedelic, space rock and sexuality. *Foxy Lady, Fire, Red*

House, Long Hot Summer Night, Gypsy Eyes and *Dolly Dagger*, for example, show a sensuality in vocal delivery and performing style that evokes an erotic intimacy which is intensified by the pounding beat and sensuous guitar style. *Gypsy Eyes* has the characteristic glissandi and bent-up notes in the guitar introduction, but the opening vocal has no supporting chords and the focus is on Hendrix's slow, sensual delivery. The overt sexuality of *Dolly Dagger* is intensified by the pounding rock beat and bass riff. The repetitive blues-like delivery of the coda and the strongly bent-up chords move towards an assertion of dominance and self-gratification which was intensified in live performance.

Spanish Castle Magic and *Are You Experienced?* exhibit comparable techniques in both vocal delivery and guitar style and again draw on a psychedelic vocabulary. Initially, it is the lyrics that point to the psychedelic. *Are You Experienced?* invites hallucinogenic exploration: 'we'll watch the sun rise from the bottom of the sea', but the focus on 'your little world', the questioning 'are you experienced' points to the need for guidance by a trained, trusted person for the first-time user of LSD.

> The underlying personality, mood, attitudes, expectations and setting in which the drug is taken have proven to be far more important as determinants of the LSD experience than with drugs such as alcohol, marijuana, barbiturates, or amphetamines . . . Because of the intensity and complexity of the experience, it can . . . be disorganising and upsetting.[32]

With Hendrix as a 'trusted' and 'experienced' guide (in the sense that he was both a loved and respected person), the changing perceptions promised by an acid trip are promised as beautiful: 'Have you ever been experienced: Well, I have. Ah, let me prove it to you.'
Spanish Castle Magic extends the *experience* itself:

> The clouds are really low and they overflow with cotton candy. . . .
> Hang on, my darling, yeah
> Hang on if you want to go

but in both songs the lyrics imply knowledge: 'candy' = the acid-impregnated sugar lump, 'stoned' = 'high', pulling on the effects of LSD, the sensation of floating. Coupled with the drive in Hendrix's guitar playing and the sheer volume of noise generated by the fuzz tone there is an implicit drowning of individual consciousness, a collective 'experience', which is reflected in the name of the band itself.

Space rock also required experience, with the form of the music depending upon comparison for symbolic communication. Its form of communication is pre-conditioned by the structures of previous symbolic transfer. Unlike Pink Floyd, however, whose space rock (e.g. *Astronomy Dominé, Set the Controls for the Heart of the Sun*) is melodically and rhythmically simple, relying on electronically produced sounds to create a dramatic realisation of the vastness and potential beauty of space, Hendrix appeared more intent on *destroying* conventional reality to constitute instead the anarchic through the mutation of sound. In the music of both bands, space rock exhibits a comparability between psychedelic rock and hallucinogenic experience: both talk of flight, of colours, of the *extra*-ordinariness of experience.

In *Up from the Skies*, Hendrix again makes use of spoken dialogue to give a more personalised address which, coupled with the use of fuzz and distortion and the upward moving figures, suggests flight and disorientation but, through experience, enjoyment:

> And I came back to find the stars misplaced
> And the smell of a world that has burned
> The smell of a world that has burned –
> I can dig it.

The songs analysed suggest that while Hendrix made use of blues resources, the Jimi Hendrix Experience was ultimately based on an immense vocabulary of sound. Volume-affecting sustain, wah-wah pedal, fuzz tone and reverb are especially important in a consideration of style, and Hendrix's experience in rock 'n' roll and rhythm and blues is apparent in the essentially rhythmic rather than lyrical guitar technique. Harmonies, melodies and lyrics appear secondary to a consideration of *effect* as what are often simple deep structures are masked by the incredible energy and forcefulness of the guitar style and the dynamics of the electronic effects.

Love or Confusion, for example, is based on the chords G, G6F and F6, the phrases are repetitive and memorable, but the overall effect is of anti-structure, due to the aural experience of the delivery, the dense sound, the feedback and distortion which move towards pure noise. *Purple Haze* is also based on a repetitive riff over a simple harmonic structure (E,G,A) but again the underlying logic of the chord progressions is transformed by Hendrix to produce a feeling of intuitive incoherence and lack of rationality through the use of fuzz tone which distorts the hammered and pulled-off notes.

While both Clapton and Hendrix's guitar styles show the influence of B.B. King there is a difference in delivery: 'where Clapton played with attack and tension, Hendrix tended to take his time and stay relaxed'[33] relying more on electronic effects to create the effect of raw energy. At the same time, Chris Welch's reviews of Clapton and Hendrix are remarkably similar. 'Hendrix: Progressive and beautiful in his ideas'; 'Clapton: Progressing with ideas and techniques'.[34] It would appear that the concept of progressiveness was strongly determined by the way in which the two musicians could work from the blues to produce new and unexpected developments. As Zappa wrote at the time: 'If you want to come up with a singular, most important trend in this new music, I think it has to be something like: it is original, composed by the people who perform it, created by them.'[35]

In terms of originality, Pink Floyd were equally influential in the development of progressive rock, but in their music there was a move towards extended compositions incorporating electronic effects. The group was initially formed by Rick Wright, keyboards, Roger Waters, bass, Nick Mason, drums and Syd Barrett, lead guitar. Barrett remained with the group until April 6, 1968 when his place was taken by Dave Gilmour.

With the line-up established, Pink Floyd played at a few dances before establishing themselves as an 'underground' group at the Spontaneous Underground, which was held every Sunday afternoon at the Marquee club in Wardour Street, Soho, from February 1966 onwards. The club was co-ordinated by Steve Stollman, an American, and very involved with free-form jazz. Though no records exist of the club, it is thought that the Floyd's first performance there was on March 13, 1966. They were already moving from a straight r&b-based style and experimenting with improvising around one chord used in a drone-like way, seeing how they could extend it. On March 27, Floyd played a number lasting half an hour against a background of red and blue lights and projected film. At that time the band were listening to such groups as Cream, the Who and Hendrix, whom they saw as formative influences on their developing style, particularly in the use of electronic feedback.[36]

In October 1966 Pink Floyd performed regularly at the London Free School's Sound/Light Workshop in Notting Hill where Joel and Toni Brown from Tim Leary's Millbrook Institute first projected slides over the band and began to develop the idea of a light show to accompany the music. On October 15, the *International Times* was launched in the London Roundhouse and Pink Floyd played to an audience of 2,000 people with moving liquid slides projected over themselves and the audience. By now the Floyd were using some unconventional musical techniques: playing the guitar with a metal cigarette lighter, rolling ball-bearings down the guitar neck to give a Bo Diddley feedback sound, and using electronic feedback in continuous controlled waves which added up to complex repeating patterns. The event generated a great deal of publicity, for both the *International Times* and Pink Floyd, who had their first interview in *Melody Maker*. Nick Jones reported: 'The Floyd need to write more of their own material– "psychedelic" versions of *Louie Louie* won't come off – but if they can incorporate their electronic prowess with some melodic and lyrical songs – getting away from dated r&b things – they could well score in the near future.'[37] The event was also covered by *The Sunday Times*, which commented on the group's throbbing music and the bizarre coloured shapes which flashed on to a screen behind the band. Brief interviews with the band were recorded, including one with Roger Waters who described their music as 'totally anarchistic. But it's co-operative anarchy . . . a complete realisation of the aims of psychedelia'.[38]

On October 31 the Floyd, together with Pete Jenner and Andrew King, set up Blackhill Enterprises as a six-way partnership to manage the group. In November they enlisted Joe Gannon to handle their lights. His slides were based on the underlying rhythm in the music, and as his hands waved over the micro-switches, different colours flashed to provide a direct link between the visual and aural effect. On December 23 the group performed at the first of the UFO Club evenings. UFO (Unlimited Freak Out) was started by John Hopkins, who ran the Sound/Light Workshop at the London Free School, where Pink Floyd were resident musicians, and who was also one of the editors of the *International Times*. The Floyd were given the contract to provide lights and sounds for the club on a percentage of the gate. At the time, they were also playing at the Marquee club where they built up an alternative following from the strictly underground one from the Free School and UFO.

UFO was, however, the focal point for Floyd's performances and as Miles points out, to really understand what caused the early music of the Floyd

> you need to be aware of the weird scene they came from. It was anarchic, innocent and didn't really take itself too seriously. . . . It was the place that Jimi Hendrix could jam with The Soft Machine before a discerning and stoned audience instead of at the 'in' clubs filled with Swinging Londoners. And it was where the Pink Floyd perfected their sound before an audience that was right in there with them, living and feeling every note.[39]

By 1967 Pink Floyd had attracted a substantial cult following, had recorded the soundtrack for, and appeared in, Peter Whitehead's film *Tonight Let's Make Love in London*, had turned professional and had two chart singles and a well-received first album.

The band's first single was a strange Syd Barrett song called *Arnold Layne*, about a transvestite who stole underclothing from washing lines. Having been persuaded by their managers to write something 'both freaky and accessible',[40] Pink Floyd saw the song rise falteringly into the lower reaches of the charts; it reached No. 20 in April 1967 and then dropped out again. *See Emily Play* was equally shortlived. These songs were to be Floyd's only singles. Essentially their musical style was difficult to contract into a three-minute record and while *Piper at the Gates of Dawn* includes songs (*Matilda Mother*, *The Gnome*, *The Scarecrow*) these are less condensed in form.

Piper at the Gates of Dawn, the Floyd's first album, was cut early in 1967 at EMI Studios, as the Beatles were recording *Sgt. Pepper* next door. Syd Barrett wrote all but one of the tracks and thematically they appear to represent the particular interests of the Floyd's underground following in their focus on science fiction, astrology, the Tarot, Tolkien, mythologies and alternative explanations. The majority of the songs are surrealistic, juxtaposing images of unicorns and kings with silver eyes and gnomes. The two songs which don't focus on Barrett's obsession with mythology are centred on the worlds beyond earth and ironically *Astronomy Dominé* and *Interstellar Overdrive* can be seen in retrospect as the base from which the Barrett-less Floyd began.

The introduction to *Astronomy Dominé* begins with distanced voices.[41] On repeated hearings it is possible to pick out the names of odd planets, departure, arrival, but even without these verbal clues the effect is of distance and space, voices announcing take-off to the world of the unknown. A fast repeated E on bass guitar works like a throbbing undertone which gradually increases in volume against Morse-like bleeps. Nick Mason's drum entry then signals the bass line which is also used as the main riff for *Interstellar Overdrive*.

The vocal line to the chorus is based on the final B/B♭ of the bass entry and has a distant, detached quality. There is little voice inflection, rather the effect is of a disembodied incantation. This is achieved by the echo effect on Barrett's voice and Rick Wright's gently moving distanced organ chords. Sudden splashes of sound on the cymbals punctuate every fourth bar, highlighting both sound and silence in the ten-bar vocal phrases. The effect is of floating, with both the vocal melodic line and the supporting guitar and organ chords moving slowly to create a mood of solemnity. Subtle changes of colour are effected by the unpredictable four-chord harmonic sequence (E/Eb/G/A) which underlies most of the piece. This works towards a disorientation of the norm,[42] and in context suggests the 'unknown':

> Lime and limpid green, a second scene, a fight between the
> blue you once knew . . .

The first planet sequence (Jupiter and Saturn, Oberon, Miranda and Titania) in particular has a gentle underlying dissonance between the E major supporting organ/guitar chords and the reiterated C# of the vocal, the almost imperceptible shift to F major in the link bar providing a momentary flash of primary colour.[43]

'Neptune, Titan, Stars can frighten' marks a change in mood as the vocal line moves to a solid dotted minim beat over a restless bass guitar before the piercing instrumental chromatic descent. The dynamic intensity of the passage propels the listener onward through space, the cymbal clashes moving the chord sequences forward as they punctuate first alternate bars, then every bar, before the more spaced-out effect of the pulsating tied minims.

The sensation is of shifting gears: initially a feeling of speed is effected by the guitar tremoloes over the continuous throb of the bass guitar. The slowed-down harmonic movement then has the effect of partial braking before the final echoing cymbal crash. A wavering A:G# on the organ continues for four bars before the entry of a pulsating high E natural on guitar which then changes to E flat as the listener is propelled further into space, evoked by the use of white sound and electronic effects.

Barrett then glissandos down for a solo break. Initially this is based on high alternating sustained notes which are bent up and sliding glissandi, fed through an echo box, before a lazy tripping sequence. This is followed by echoing strums across the chords which are distanced by the use of overlay and echo. Underneath the organ holds the supporting harmonies, while the bass guitar continues the three in a bar throbbing pulse (see Example 7).

The instrumental continues with increasing intensity as the basic chord structure (E/Eb/G/A) is overlaid with electronically dominated noise. In the context of space, the connotations are explorative: the instrumental collage, pre-recorded effects and improvised solo lines create an aural experience of the cosmos through timbre and colour while the established logic of the chord sequence provides an underlying sense of control.[44] Distanced voices, white noise and increasing electronic effects then move the listener further into space before the vocal entry. This picks up on the rhythm of the 'Neptune Titan' phrase of the first chorus, the 'flicker, flicker, flicker, blam' coloured by an echoing 'pow' and hissing white sound which preface the questioning 'Scare Dan Dare Who's there?' and the second entry of the tremolo descending chord sequence.

Finally the coda takes up the initial lines of the first verse: 'lime and limpid green' tying the imagery to the sounds of space themselves, the sounds which 'surround the icy waters underground'. Based on an A drone over a sinuous organ line the vocals evoke the unchanging nature of space. This time, however, the established chord sequence changes. Instead of E/Eb/G/A, the first sixteen bars are based on D minor/F major. This is answered by twenty bars on D major/D minor/F major, with the final entry on D major bringing a sense of overall control in its resolution on a perfect cadence.[45]

Astronomy Dominé quickly became an established part of Pink Floyd's performing repertoire as well featuring on the live recording for their double album *Ummagumma* (1969). Even so, the recordings on *Piper at the Gates of Dawn* and *Ummagumma* separate the music from the visual context of the moving slides and flashing lights which accompanied live performances of *Astronomy Dominé* at the time.

> After a whole night of frolicking and festivities and acid came the celebration of the dawn . . . Syd's eyes blazed as his notes soared up into the strengthening light . . . then came the rebirth of energy . . . As Roger Waters commented: 'It's not difficult to convert the audience to this presentation. It's very beautiful to watch. It takes them straight away. It's so different. It's like . . . it's impossible to say what it's like . . . For us the most important thing is to be visual'.[46]

The question thus arises as to whether *Astronomy Dominé* can be read as a psychedelic track without the accompanying light show.

At the time of its release in August 1967, American groups – The Grateful Dead, Big Brother and the Holding Company, Jefferson Airplane and the Quicksilver Messenger Service – had already pioneered acid rock. Allen Ginsberg, who had been one of the promoters of the Albert Hall poetry reading in January 1967, had launched the world's first Human Be-In in Haight-Ashbury.

Example 7 Astronomy Dominé

Many of those present were graduates from Ken Kesey's notorious acid tests. Begun in August 1965, the tests continued until L.S.D. was declared illegal in October 1966, by which time it was estimated that ten thousand – the same number as the park celebrants – had ingested the drug in sugar lumps, punch, coffee or cookies. It was at these intensive social environments, initially in a garage and later moving to the Fillmore Auditorium, that stroboscopic light shows were allegedly invented and the whole pulsating minutiae of electronic party gadgets perfected.[47]

In England a similar environment was that of John Hopkins' UFO Club. Here *Astronomy Dominé* provided a musical voyage into the unknown in its creation of a new reality based on swirling colours and dense improvisatory passages. While the Floyd stressed that 'We don't call ourselves a psychedelic group or say that we play psychedelic pop music'[48] they also drew attention to the need to *know* that particular forms of music, such as their own space rock, were played when 'tripping'. So the association of acid with lights and a spontaneous form of music became identified with *Astronomy Dominé* and *Interstellar Overdrive*, which have now become classics.

In the psychedelic music in England which developed within a specific London environment, long, improvisatory passages and electronically produced sound effects resonated with stroboscopic lighting to bring about a freedom of feeling analogous to the effect of acid: the 'piling up of new sensations', the associations with changed perceptions and colour. Within *Astronomy Dominé* the electronic mutation of sound, the huge overwhelming textures, the sinuous *tripping* of the lead guitar and organ around the basic notes and the incantatory, mesmeric effect of Wright's voice reflect the state of mind on a hallucinogenic trip. In particular, the dip shapes in the guitar solo create a strong feeling of floating around the beat and this is reinforced by the lazy meandering around the notes, again suggestive of a state of tripping where the fixed point takes on a new reality. Throughout the song, the use of repetition both in the chord sequence and in the vocals works towards a feeling of obsessiveness. The chord sequence moves against any formal organisation and, apart from the pause, which separates the two parts of the song to create a feeling of stopped time, and the final cadence, there is no real resolution. Instead there is a movement towards a disorientation of the norm, and as in *Purple Haze*, there is a total sense of absorption within the sound itself.

Returning to the question of whether *Astronomy Dominé* can be read as a psychedelic track without the accompanying light show, the inbuilt codes discussed earlier would suggest that there was a homology between the sounds and the experiences encountered on a trip. 'Space rock', with its exploration of alternative experiences, locks into the psychedelic, the effects of acid and the emphasis on being *spaced* out, the escape from a rational time sense.

Barrett had become increasingly unpredictable over the course of 1967. Occasionally he would disappear and David O'List from the Nice would take his place. At other times he would go on stage and just play the same chord all evening while the rest of the group tried to cover up. In January 1968 Dave Gilmour was invited to join the group, making it a five-piece. The official statement was that the Floyd were augmenting to explore new instruments and add further experimental dimensions to their sound. In reality they were trying to find a way of keeping Barrett on as a writer but without having to rely on his performing. Barrett's condition worsened, however, and on April 6 he left the group.[49]

While Pink Floyd's performing ability remained unimpaired by Barrett's departure, inasmuch as Gilmour could play guitar in Syd's style and Roger Waters could sing, the problem remained of what to put on top of the bass if it couldn't be Syd's weird lyrics. Having worked extensively in building complex musical structures from a simple rock base, the most obvious path was to concentrate on electronics and presentation and to develop the style of music with which they had become associated. Using *Astronomy Dominé* and *Interstellar Overdrive* as the basis for a musical exploration of sound and light, Floyd moved increasingly towards dramatic extended compositions.

Set the Controls for the Heart of the Sun is typical of Floyd's music at this time in its melodic and rhythmic simplicity. Like *Astronomy Dominé* there is an irresistible sense of movement which is set in motion initially by the bass and picked up by the drums and organ. Again the piece features barely audible whispered lyrics and occasional sinuous runs on the organ. Unlike *Astronomy Dominé*, *Set the Controls for the Heart of the Sun* has no lyrics apart from the repeated title line, and the piece is above all mysterious. The first of the three 'movements' is based on spaced-out organ chords and gentle discords and evokes a mood of uncertainty. This contrasts with the second movement which is far more discordant and rhythmically energetic. Tension is generated through electronic screams and off-beat piano chords. The third and final movement starts with what sounds like a diminishing explosion which moves towards grandiose organ chords, an orchestral chorus and strings to end with two minutes of serene beauty.

The idea of an extended piece was carried through to *Ummagumma*, which was released as a double album on EMI's new underground label, Harvest, in October 1969. The first half of the album, recorded at Mother's Club, Birmingham and the College of Commerce, Manchester, included live versions of *Astronomy Dominé*, *Careful with that Axe, Eugene*, *Set the Controls for the Heart of the Sun* and *A Saucerful of Secrets*. This second album was experimental, with each member of the band having half a side to experiment with as they wished.

By 1970, tape effects were becoming an integral part of Floyd's music and live performances were also accompanied by complex sound systems. While many accused Floyd of turning their backs on their underground roots, in that their music needed complex and expensive technology, their musical themes remained essentially those which had been at the core of counter-cultural philosophy: space travel, the nature of time and the inner world of thoughts and feelings. *Atom Heart Mother* (1970) was again considered by the group to be an experiment rather than a new direction and *Meddle* (1971) was equally thought to be only a relative success. Side one was composed of songs; side two was an extended composition called *Echoes*. The construction is similar to that of *Atom Heart Mother* in that it runs through several movements. This time, however, the movements are sufficiently different to create a sense of exploring a varied musical landscape.

While the piece overall is not especially innovative, relying on the slow 4-tempo and repetitive melody line that had become characteristic of many of Floyd's songs, the lyrics are impressionistic and with the restless mood of the music reinforce the feeling of movement and flight. Originally entitled *Return to the Sun of Nothing*, there is the suggestion of space, especially in the use of the Binson echo unit which creates the particularly strong harmonics with which the piece opens. At the same time, the use of electronically synthesised sound, while creating the feeling of space, could also evoke psychedelic exploration or a seascape. Within the total context of the piece, the lyrics suggest the latter – 'the echo of a distant tide comes willowing across the sand' – which is possibly the reason why Pink Floyd changed the original title to *Echoes*.

Although *Echoes* is sufficiently dramatic to stand on its own, without either film footage or the elaborate light and firework show that had accompanied its performance at the Crystal Palace on May 15, 1971, the use of the repetitive melody line and constant electronic effects suggests, nevertheless, that the Floyd were locked within a particular compositional framework. *Atom Heart Mother* and *A Saucerful of Secrets* could be described simply in terms of their technical proficiency: beautifully put together but overall a composite of electronic effects. The Floyd were equally conscious that they were simply 'zig-zagging their way about',[50] and that what was needed was a synthesis of their two main compositional approaches: the closed song (e.g. *Arnold Layne*, *See Emily Play*, *Lucifer Sam*, *Matilda Mother*, etc.) and the open piece (eg *Astronomy Dominé*, *Ummagumma*, *Set the Controls for the Heart of the Sun*).

The synthesis was achieved in *Dark Side of the Moon*, which is analysed in depth in Chapter 6: the basic theme provides the discipline and focus through interlinked songs, while its extended exploration of madness allows for dramatic presentation through such devices as sound collages and electronic effects.

With Pink Floyd's increasing use of taped effects the feeling of sponta-neity which characterises Hendrix's and Clapton's lead breaks is missing. Despite this there are parallels: all three bands focus attention on the *sound* of the music and while Hendrix and Clapton's development of the blues focuses on producing new and unexpected developments particularly in the guitar breaks, Floyd's originality and creative exploration lies in their use of electronic effects in both their psychedelic and space rock compositions. In all three bands originality, innovation and creativity is instantly recognisable as authentic, as having developed from a specific musical starting point. As Middleton and Muncie point out: 'There's an internal logic to the development of musical codes. Certain materials impose certain routes . . .'.[51]

Progressive rock, as composed and performed by Cream, Hendrix, and Pink Floyd, was constituted by specific musical features which show a sense of development and originality from a base style. Clapton, Baker and Bruce had all come out of the British rhythm and blues movement; Pink Floyd began as a rhythm and blues band and Hendrix was equally conversant with the style. Pink Floyd's interest in electronic feedback techniques is similar to that of Hendrix, but whereas the former moved increasingly to studio-based taped sounds and complex electronic equipment, the Jimi Hendrix sound was characterised more by individualised distortion of his own guitar through wah-wah pedal and fuzz tone. Electronics appear to reinforce his already personalised, physical feeling for the guitar sound itself. In contrast, Floyd mingled voices, guitars, organ, drums, timpani with electronic and stereophonic effects to create elaborate sound collages. Clapton initially shared Hendrix's interest in guitar electronics, using wah-wah pedal, fuzz and reverb on *Disraeli Gears* but on the whole he preferred to experiment with different guitars to obtain new sounds rather than distorting the sound of one or two. All three bands, however, focus on the development of musical ideas through extensive improvisations.

Progressive rock was of particular importance to the counter-culture, who saw it not only as a major source of communication but also as symbolically representing their own search for alternative cognitive and social modes beneath and outside the dominant culture.[52] It was thought to have a message, to say things of political and cultural significance; it was experimental and focused on an immediacy of experience (which is reflected both in the apparent spontaneity in improvisation and the emphasis on live performance and festivals), and was often drug-centred (if not always drug-induced) and offered heightened awareness of the world.

Progressive rock could bridge social and national differences and, especially in the USA, racial differences. While festivals in particular reflect this immediate search for the experience of community, the LP, and in particular the concept album, was also recognised as providing a means to a mutuality of consciousness whereby the individual could be confirmed as one part of a collective whole.

In many ways the acceptance of recordings is ironic in that the underground had originally come out strongly against commercialisation, separating themselves ideologically from the circumstances in which music was made.[53] Pink Floyd had originated as an underground band who were seen as part of a total environment. Their music and light shows had been orientated towards a collective process of experience and members of the UFO Club saw themselves as a cult, anxious to exclude outsiders. It was possibly Floyd's performances at other venues, in particular the Round-house, the Marquee and the highly publicised Commonwealth Institute concert that focused attention on the profit-making potential of the underground. It was inevitable that record companies would be attracted, and when in 1967 *Arnold Layne* and *See Emily Play* reached the charts, Floyd joined Cathy McGowan, Chrissie Shrimpton, Michael Rainey, David Ormsby-Gore and the Beatles in a mural of 'Swinging London' in Madame Tussaud's Waxworks.

It was, perhaps, less surprising that Clapton and Hendrix should attract such an immediate and extensive following. Rock 'n' roll, in Britain, had been primarily a guitar-based music and while America made it a vehicle for teen idols who did not play their own instruments, Britain favoured the guitar heroes: Buddy Holly, the Everly Brothers, and Eddie Cochran. Gene Vincent. The success of the Shadows depended on their followers, who identified with the image of three young men wielding guitars, and most British pop groups in the mid-sixties featured guitars in both their sound and visual images.

The first British blues boom was contemporary with the rock 'n' roll upsurge of 1964–5, but had never really taken off. The second, however, found an immediate audience in the underground clubs and the expanding college/university circuit. Many of the leading performers, including Cream, had originally been members of the first wave of groups, including John Mayall's Bluesbreakers and Alexis Korner's Blues Inc. Together with Jimi Hendrix, the blues movement was given a high profile in music magazines and in 1967–8 numerous groups sprang up, including Fleetwood Mac, Free, Jethro Tull and the Jeff Beck Group.

So there was a certain inevitability in the fact that Cream's single, *I Feel Free* should become an instant chart success. Jimi Hendrix also attracted wide press coverage and his singles were launched to critical acclaim. At the same time, *I Feel Free* and *See Emily Play*[54] could be considered as fulfilling the criteria of pop: 'is it catchy, melodic, entertaining?'[55] and both Cream and Floyd were quick to come out against the power of the record companies, in particular the criteria of 'take something out if it doesn't fit the three minute space available'. As Clapton pointed out:

> To get any good music in a space of two or three minutes requires working to a formula and that part of the pop scene really leaves me cold . . . The whole music scene in Britain is ruled by the charts and people are brainwashed into thinking that the number one record represents the best music available . . . our management has come to realise that unless we are allowed to do what we want to do, we can kick up a bigger stink about it than them.[56]

True to their word, Cream released no more singles, other than those culled from albums by the record company. Floyd and Hendrix also moved to LPs, which allowed for greater freedom of expression.

It was, of course, critical that audiences shared the bands' stand against singles, and it could be considered that *Melody Maker*'s emphasis on *musicianship* was important in promoting the idea of artistry linked to LPs. In 1967 Clapton was voted top British musician, Cream were voted fourth group, a good showing behind the Beatles and the Jimi Hendrix Experience, considering the paucity of Cream's chart successes to date, but probably due to Baker and Bruce's previous reputation in the Graham Bond Organisation and Clapton's personal following, established when in John Mayall's Bluebreakers. *Disraeli Gears* reached No. 5 in the UK album charts: *Wheels of Fire* went gold in America even before it was shipped. In 1968 Cream were voted into every available top slot in the music polls both as a band and as individual instrumentalists. Clapton topped the *Melody Maker* poll in the British and world musician section and in 1969 *Goodbye* topped the charts on both sides of the Atlantic, staying in the UK top ten for thirteen weeks.

Hendrix was equally successful with *Are You Experienced?* coming thirteenth in the top-selling albums. The double LP *Electric Ladyland* topped the American album charts a few weeks after Cream in 1968. While Floyd's *Saucerful of Secrets* was greeted with critical acclaim, it was not until the release of *Atom Heart Mother* that the band achieved any real commercial success (other than with the two early singles). *Atom Heart Mother* reached No. 1 in the UK charts, but was eclipsed by *Dark Side of the Moon*, which provided the group with their first US No. 1 and took up permanent residency in the UK charts for more than two years.

The three bands had not only a commercial success but had also found an appropriate form in the LP medium, which was seen as making possible the collectivity of musical experience essential to the thinking of the counter-culture. The success of all three bands on both sides of the Atlantic seemed to indicate that the disc could guarantee that progressive rock could be effective across all frontiers, that individual listeners could feel at one with the counter-cultural community regardless of distance. The mass of buyers (vital to the top-of-the-pops chart successes) could now be redefined. They were no longer manipulated by the record promoters, the disc jockeys and the musical press, but were themselves a key factor in the collectivity of experience.

3   The Beatles

You want a piece of music to encapsulate the period it was written in, and *Sgt. Pepper* does seem to do that.[1]

It was the closest Western Civilisation had come to unity since the Congress of Vienna in 1815. . . . At the time *Sgt. Pepper* was released I happened to be driving across country on Interstate 80. In each city I stopped . . . the melodies wafted in from some far-off transistor radio or portable hi-fi. It was the most amazing thing I've ever heard. For a brief moment, the irreparably fragmented consciousness of the West was unified, at least in the minds of the young.[2]

When the Beatles' work as a whole is viewed in retrospect, *Rubber Soul* and *Revolver* will stand as their major contributions. When the slicks and tricks of production on this new album no longer seem unusual and the compositions are stripped to their musical and lyrical essentials, *Sergeant Pepper* will be the Beatles baroque – an elaboration without improvement.[3]

These conflicting responses to *Sgt. Pepper* focus attention both on the music and on its historical and social contextualisation. If Kenneth Tynan could claim that the Album was 'a decisive moment in the history of Western Civilisation',[4] and William Mann that it encapsulated 'the period it was written in',[5] then Richard Goldstein's observation that 'the Beatles have given us a package of special effects, dazzling but ultimately fraudulent . . . an obsession with the surrogate magic of production, and a new sarcasm masquerading as cool . . . a dangerously dominant sense of what is chic'[6] equally highlights the summer of '67 itself when so many of the radical issues of the counter-culture had apparently become subsumed by the commercialism of Carnaby Street and when such underground bands as Cream, Pink Floyd, and Jimi Hendrix could feature in the Top Twenty.[7]

In many ways 1967 was a microcosm of the struggle of the decade it divided, in its interplay of action and reaction, liberalisation and repression. Britain had finally passed the Sexual Offences and Abortion Acts. Exactly one month after the release of *Sgt. Pepper*, the famous editorial by Rees-

Mogg 'Who Breaks a Butterfly on a Wheel?' appeared in *The Times*. Some three weeks later the same paper published an advertisement advocating the legalisation of marijuana, to which the Beatles were signatories. However, it is difficult to resist the suspicion that any doctrine that leads to greater freedom of self-expression and individualism among the governed, but which is not sanctioned by the governors, must needs be repressed, and LSD was also made illegal in the Dangerous Drugs Act. Pirate radio was also suppressed, but at the same time that *Rolling Stone* appeared, the Youth International Party was formed, the Pentagon was exorcised and the Beatles embraced transcendental meditation.

Into this seemingly confused dialogue *Sgt. Pepper* was launched and hailed by many as an expression of optimism. As Allen Ginsberg recalled in the 1987 TV programme 'Twenty Years Ago Today', 'there was here an exclamation of joy, the rediscovery of joy and what it was to be alive . . . It was actually a cheerful look around the world: the first time, I would say on a mass scale'. Despite the murder of Che Guevara, the race riots in Detroit and the gathering discontent at universities both in America and England, *Sgt. Pepper* seemed at the time to exemplify a mood of 'getting better'. 'Holes' were being 'fixed', love would still be there at 64 and the Band promised to 'turn you on'.

As Chapter 2 pointed out, the question that arises is the extent to which the *Sgt. Pepper* album merely constituted optimistic escapism, a 'distraction' from the demands of reality, or whether it 'gave voice to a feeling that the old ways were out',[8] and set the agenda for a counter-cultural response in England in terms both of cultural themes and of music.

Certainly the opening track encapsulates the mood of optimism that seemed to characterise 1967. There is a strong sense of togetherness and communality. The mood is buoyant and interactive, drawing perhaps on Paul McCartney's recent experience as a member of the Monterey Festival Board, an event which had established a new set of relationships between performer and audience and a new idea of the possibilities of rock, with particular attention to San Francisco psychedelia. This time, however, there is a particularly English emphasis in the Edwardian figure of Sgt. Pepper himself. The effect is to place the music within the context of the military bandstand with its attendant mood of light-hearted festivity. The delivery is extrovert and replete with military cliché.

The use of sound collage – crowd noises, the band tuning up – functions both as a narrative source and as a psychological way of creating a mood of shared festivity. The audience, both as part of the recording and as listeners, are drawn together and once established as a community can 'sit back and let the evening flow'. At the same time, the track calls up past associations. The use of the high-volume, intense distorted guitar sound, the tremolo effects, the rhythmically reiterated pitches which alternate with wide melodic leaps, the sharp rhythmic guitar chords and the syncopated bass guitar line are reminiscent of *Taxman*. There is a sense of shared identity:

the audience recognise the style and are confident that they are 'in the hands of the Beatles'.

At surface level this is an optimistic track which juxtaposes the old-world military band with the contemporary sound of the rock group. It is debatable whether this juxtaposition is one of traditional stability with contemporary uncertainty; whether the new takes on strength from the old through role play and borrowed uniforms; whether this harks back to the popular, fun-loving image of the Beatles themselves or whether it is a reconstruction of the mood of the underground itself. At the time of its release, the Beatles were regular visitors to the UFO Club with its endless 'mixture of bands, poets, jugglers . . . hash, sweat',[9] light shows and 'strange garbs . . . the more outrageous the better'.[10] Within the album's overall theme of communal experience, the ragbag of images, Mr. Kite, Rita, Lucy, Billy Shears, Sgt. Pepper himself, pull on the cultural politics of the psychedelic left: 'Eradicate the Victorian Depression ethic of virtuous sacrifice and remind the world that love must be a constantly original and divine word.'[11]

The central figure of Sgt. Pepper resonates with the ethos of the underground in its refusal of this 'virtuous sacrifice'. By wearing the uniform of the past within the context of a psychedelically charged album, Sgt. Pepper undercuts traditional values and the military man becomes yet another showman, a figure of fun.

The concept of old versus new is established by the juxtaposition of the military band with the 'pop group', the imitative Edwardian-style band music contrasting with the rock structure of the verse with its I, II–IV–V progression. The flattened third and seventh on 'Lonely Hearts Club' reflects back on the audience themselves, the people who have come to hear the band who have themselves been playing together since 'twenty years ago today'. There is, nevertheless, an underlying optimism as the supporting harmonies move back to the major on the word 'Band' and the song overall is characterised by a sense of mounting enthusiasm. The last verse, in particular, with its crowd effects and vocal cheers, establishes a mood of classic vaudeville which is harmonically reinforced by the I–II–III music hall cliché which established Paul as master of ceremonies introducing the first act, 'the one and only Billy Shears'.

Billy Shears/Ringo Starr gets by with 'a little help from my friends', but needs 'somebody to love'. Melodically the song might well have come earlier in the Beatles' career; its simple, narrow-ranged repetitive tune evokes the pristine quality of such songs as *From Me To You*, *She Loves You*, *All My Loving*, (1963) *And I Love Her*, and *Can't Buy Me Love* (1964) where images and memorable phrases had a 'lack of contrivance'.[12] As Charlie Gillett points out, by 1966

the emotionally expressive rock and roll singers of *Love Me Do* had given way to people apparently ready to try any style known to man, contemporary eastern, nineteenth century vaudeville. But while it seemed that McCartney would be happy seeing how many different things he could do well, John Lennon moved with determination back to music that expressed feelings, simple, repetitive, but personal; *All You Need is Love, Revolution, Come Together.*[13]

Written by Lennon/McCartney and sung by Ringo Starr, *With a Little Help from my Friends* has a strongly repetitive melody. There are few studio tricks, with the exception of the double-tracking on the chorus, and the sentiments are explicit despite a certain ambiguity in the rhyming incantation 'I get by, I get high, I can try' with its passing reference to LSD. The simplicity of the melody is matched by the directness of the words but instead of the earlier buoyancy of the 1963–4 songs, there is a mood of inadequacy. This, however, is Ringo singing, 'the least talented, the least articulate, "inferior" member of the group'.[14] This inadequacy is reflected particularly in the question/answer dialogue in the third verse:

Would you believe in a love at first sight?
Yes, I'm certain that it happens all the time

where Ringo's solo contrasts with the duetted response to reflect back on the separateness/togetherness theme of the opening track.

The chorus is more positive. Initially Ringo sings on his own, but is joined by McCartney on 'I'm gonna try with a little help from my friends' to give a sense of support. Within a concept album the positioning of the last chorus takes on added significance in that it helps to fix the meaning of the next track, *Lucy in the Sky with Diamonds*. Ringo's friends *might* have helped by taking him along to the entertaining Mr. Kite, but 'I get high with a little help from my friends' is given a specific meaning in the psychedelic coding of *Lucy in the Sky with Diamonds*, a song which partially resolves the uncertainty and needs of the lonely person by evoking the colour, freedom and beauty of love experienced on a trip. As Joel Fort writes:

Psychedelic drugs . . . do not produce or encourage sexual desire and do not excite the sexual organs, but they can 'profoundly enhance the quality of sexual acts that occur between people who would in any case have had intercourse.'. . . Strong emotional bonds or positive feelings for each other; changes in time (and other sensory) perception; unusual genital sensations; diminished inhibitions and symbolic overtones can be part of an LSD experience and will in some circumstances produce a mystical or ecstatic sexual union which may seem endless. The presence or absence of companions, acquaintances, friends or loved ones is certainly an important determinant. If warmth, reassurance and knowledgeable guidance are provided, bad experiences . . . are less likely to occur or be bothersome.[15]

'I get by with a little help from my friends, I get high with a little help from my friends, I'm gonna try with a little help from my friends' provides, then, a reassuring setting.

For acid wasn't just a private pleasure, it was a revolutionary tool for inspiring within common clay a cornucopia of poems, moods, paintings and music . . . it could unite the world and achieve Nirvana. Acid was a crash course in the solution of that age old occidental problem of alienation. LSD said 'We are one'.[16]

Preceded by the Beatles' earlier psychedelic single, *Strawberry Fields Forever* (1967), there is knowledgeable support and, despite Lennon's denial of the encoded reference to LSD in the title, the words and music of *Lucy* evoke, for the initiated at least, the heightened sensations experienced on a 'trip'.[17]

Everyday experience:

Picture yourself in a boat on the river

is transformed into an evocative sign through the intensification of the unusual visual experience:

With tangerine trees and marmalade skies

The singer takes on the role of experienced user and in the verse leads the novice – to whom the effects are most unfamiliar and who therefore might be expected to suffer most from drug-induced anxiety – into a changed reality. By learning 'the culture from older users in conversation [new users] are thus protected from the dangers of panic or "flipping out".[18]

In the context of an LSD experience, the gentleness of the pulse of *Lucy* is reassuring, and with the electronic distancing of the voice provides 'a kind of *denotational* relationship to physical experiences: blurring of images and of speech, and unnaturally bright colours are both, said to be characteristic of hallucinatory conditions'.[19]

The waltz tune itself 'undulates around the third of the scale (with dreamy flat sixths and sevenths in the accompaniment',[20] while the bright tinkly scoring evokes the unnatural brightness of 'the girl with kaleidoscope eyes'. The tonality appears equally insubstantial as it shifts from a modal A up to Bb and along with the new filtered sound and the synthesised chord effect there is the suggestion of hallucinatory images – the 'cellophane flowers', the 'newspaper taxis' which take the novice/listener upwards to the ephemeral 'girl with the sun in her eyes'.

The dreamy waltz, evoking the positive experiences of the trip, is then broken by the apparent contradiction in mood of the 'Lucy' refrain. The brief, unremitting phrases and the basic conception of the rhythm (regular beat plus syncopation) hark back to the Beatles' earlier rock style (*I Wanna Be Your Man, Drive My Car*). The timbres are clean and unblurred and by reference to the scoring of the verse suggest 'normal' experience, real life. In the frame of reference of the song the exuberant refrain suggests the mood of self-assurance gained from a good trip. According to Neville, 'non-acid takers regard the L.S.D. trip as a remarkable flight from reality, where as cautious devotees feel they've flown *into reality*'[21] and while the return of the refrain as a coda interspersed with the equivocal 'Ah' might suggest a slight sense of loss as the music fades out, the lack of finality is reassuring. The experience can be repeated.

While the precise meaning of *Lucy* remains conjectural, it could be argued that the conjunction of electronically manipulated timbres, the unlikely modulations 'narrow down and fix the signified of the final collage'.[22] The lyrics leave little doubt that the song focuses hallucinogenic experience. Contextualised by McCartney's 'grand announcement that he took LSD [but] . . . couldn't be responsible if other people blindly followed his example',[23] Lennon's arrival at Epstein's party in Sussex 'in his psychedelic Rolls-Royce . . . with lots of LSD [when] many well-known show business personalities were turned on to the drug for the first time'[24] and Epstein's own quote in *Queen* magazine that the 'new mood in the country . . . has originated through hallucinatory drugs. I am wholeheartedly on its side',[25] *Lucy* was quickly perceived as more than a simple comic-book flight of fantasy.

> Thousands of pimply-faced high-school kids soon deduced that *Sgt. Pepper* was LSD inspired. Those that didn't were enlightened by *Time* magazine. The cult heroes were popularising acid and psychedelia, and inevitably, the initiates were going to follow . . . Kids who had never smoked a marijuana cigarette in their lives were dropping acid and taking speed . . . Drug use had caught up with the drug orientation of rock and the fusion of the two was beginning to take place in the consciousness of a generation.[26]

In *Apple to the Core* Aspinall, road manager and personal assistant, had written that *Sgt. Pepper* was 'the culmination of our acid days',[27] attaching a certain social prominence to being the first to take LSD, 'as if the distinction of being an early initiate implies that you were an artistic or cultural leader of the time'.

> John Dunbar is convinced that they weren't trendsetters. 'The Beatles, all of them, are very naive in many ways. I saw them influenced by all sorts of nonsense a number of times. In general, they went along with everything that was happening in the sixties. They made fine music, sure. But their names were linked to acid, and it was assumed that they were leaders in this field too.'[28]

However, as McCabe and Schonfield point out, 'Even if they weren't trendsetters, for much of the youth in the sixties, the Beatles were the "four wise men". They were the heralds of an alternative culture.'[29] At the time of its release, stream-of-consciousness poetry and the electronic treatment of sound had been so widely copied that they had become a norm in themselves,[30] to suggest, through music, an LSD experience. In this, *Lucy* was not specially innovative. The song drew and enlarged on the hallucinogenic vocabulary of other songs of the period: Dylan's *Mr Tambourine Man*; Donovan's *Mellow Yellow* and *Sunshine Superman*; Jefferson Airplane's *White Rabbit*; the Rolling Stones' *Something Happened to Me Yesterday* and their own *Strawberry Fields Forever*.[31]

The imagery in *Lucy*, its poetically comic-book flowers, trees and people, also link the song to the Pop Art movement of the early sixties and to underground posters of the period. 'Breezes', 'Unicorn', 'Middle Earth', 'Pot Rally' and 'John Lennon', issued by Effective Communications Arts Limited make use of the same bright colours as those evoked in *Lucy*, 'Night Ferry' focuses the 'girl with kaleidoscope eyes', while 'Pete B.own: the first real poetry band' dreams up images not dissimilar to those on the *Sgt. Pepper* sleeve. All five posters refer to hallucinogenic experience.

While the images in *Lucy* 'could come as easily from Edward Lear as from the experience of drugs', and Lennon himself claimed that the title of the song is not an anagram for LSD but was taken from a drawing his son did at school, his two books on Joycean punning (*In His Own Write* and *A Spaniard in the Works*) illustrate 'to the point of hilarity that one meaning denies the presence of another, which it has hidden inside, only to all strangers and the police'.[32] As Richard Poirier writes:

> 'the Beatles have the distinction in their work of *knowing* that this is how they see and feel these things and of enjoying the knowledge . . . and at least four of the songs on the *Sgt. Pepper* album are concerned with taking a 'trip' or 'turning on'. *A Little Help From My Friends*, *Lucy in the Sky with Diamonds*, *Fixing a Hole* and *A Day in the Life* with a good chance of a fifth in *Getting Better*.[33]

Getting Better expresses anger and frustration with the establishment – the school rebel, the angry young man. The introduction establishes a rebellious mood as guitar staccato chords on the subdominant conflict with a piercing pedal reiteration on the dominant. At the same time, the bouncy rhythm and falsetto 'What did you say?' and 'It can't get worse!' suggest that the attack on authority:

'I used to get mad at my school'

and self-denunication:

'I used to be cruel to my woman'
shouldn't be taken too seriously, and this somewhat flippant mood is reinforced by background comments: 'Though I can't complain!'

At one level the song develops the Lennon/McCartney recognition through music that the need for love is historical and recurrent, even if the 'songs they wrote, like the harmonies they sang, derived freshness from a perpetual contest, even clash, of two wholly unalike minds. John, with his sarcasm, ruthlessly cut back on the cloying sweetness to which Paul was often prone.'[34] Lennon's sense of irony pierces any sentimentality, the stepped falsetto barber-shop quartet effect on 'Better, better, better', the tongue-in-cheek 'It can't get any worse', the simple harmonic treatment reminiscent of music-hall style. So despite the stabilising effect of the repetitive rhythmic structure and the upward tendency of the melodic line, it seems somewhat naive to place too much credibility on the statement that things are improving simply because 'he's' met 'her'.

The 'getting better' sequence is more laid back, the rhythm is relaxed and focused by 'you gave me the word', takes on an alternative meaning.

> L.S.D. demands more than marijuana. You can keep your plastic job and then come home at night and turh on and make love better and enjoy music better and enjoy your dinner better and enjoy your friends better . . . but L.S.D. requires a change of mind.[35]

'Getting better' refers to the before and after – the frustrations expressed through the boogie rhythmed tune contrast with the light-hearted simplicity of the diatonic refrain to resonate with yet another aspect of counter-cultural politics, 'perhaps its greatest innovation – the element of play, the mocking of conventions ("it can't get worse"), the laughter which counter-acts the fury and the loneliness and frustration',[36] the turning on to an alternative and 'better' experience. As Neville writes,

> Sex is pure when it's playful . . . Children explore in indiscriminate and anarchistic fashion all the erotic potentialities of the human body. Sounds like the sex habits of the Underground, which is still, like the children, narcissistic and guiltless . . . The Underground is turning sex back into play.[37]

Fixing a Hole carries the LSD experience one stage further.

> I'm fixing a hole where the rain gets in
> And stops my mind from wandering
> Where it will go

The drug-taking implications of 'fixing' are given strong musical support by coming on the first beat of the bar on the key note to create the sense of security needed if there is to be a positive enhancement of sensibility. 'If the individual is in a comfortable and familiar environment such as his own living room, he is much less likely to experience drug troubles.'[38]

Lilting fourths in the vocal line are softened by descending flattened sevenths; the end of the first strain floats upwards, always just off the beat to suggest a loosening between the self and the environment: 'mood changes or swings can occur and sometimes intense pleasurable or esthetic experience'.[39]

The change in mood in the middle section equally suggests a reflection of hallucinogenic experience. Having been 'freed', the lyricism of the verse changes to a diatonic F major with sharpened sevenths and a strong repetitive vocal line. As Joel Fort observes:

> Throughout the experience the normal individual has insight, is fully aware that he is experiencing a drug effect, and is able to respond to the

reality of telephones, doorbells etc., although he will usually be less inclined to do so because of a feeling that these things are not so important.[40]

The song then returns to its original lilting melody. With each return of the refrain, the texture becomes fuller as if to establish the added dimension of the LSD experience. The 'holes', the 'cracks' have been fixed, the 'establishment' kept out and the singer, Paul, is free to explore the changes in time and perception characteristic of hallucinogenics.

In some ways it is paradoxical that Paul, as the last Beatle to take LSD, should sing *Fixing a Hole*.

His cautious reluctance was finally broken down as the group began recording its acid-inspired masterpiece, *Sgt. Pepper* early in 1967 . . . Lennon rarely misses an opportunity to put down McCartney and even Aspinall because they were slower than he to capitulate to the hallucinogenic powers of the drug. One thing is certain. After his initial experiences with LSD, Paul McCartney became convinced that *Sgt. Pepper*, with its many drug connotations, was a work of great artistic and social significance.[41]

The 'Hey hey hey' which precedes the final guitar chord suggests another instance of Lennon's sarcastic wit. There is both a musical reference to the innocence of the early Beatles songs, the characteristic 'Yeah, yeah, yeah' and a neat 'put down': 'He's finally done it !'

In many ways *Fixing a Hole* complements *Lucy*. Both explore the potential of LSD for changing perceptions and the musical coding of the two songs suggests affirmation. In both songs there are contrasts between the lyrical and more rock-inspired sections that have much in common with the structuring of Californian acid rock. *Fixing a Hole* floats above a secure diatonic base; *Lucy* asserts an innocence and colour lacking in everyday life, a solution to the problem of alienation and aloneness preferable to the faceless figure of the establishment 'man from the motor trade' evoked in *She's Leaving Home*.

She's Leaving Home is a simple narrative ballad which questions traditional family relationships. In common with other social protest songs of the period, the song points to the alienation of youth from consumerism and materialism, which were recognised as repressive and constraining. The Kinks' *Dead End Street*, the Stones' *Mother's Little Helper*, Manfred Mann's *Semi-Detached Suburban Mr. Jones*, the Beatles' *Nowhere Man* and *Eleanor Rigby* question and reject the values of the dominant culture by laying bare the loneliness of the individual.

However, while the songs expressed the problems, they offered no direct solutions and the individuals within the narrative were often inarticulate and haunting images of loneliness who were constantly castigated by an indifferent world. In contrast, the politics of the counter-culture was to actively set up the 'international, equisexual, tribal, nomadic lifestyle implicit in the Movement'.[42] In this light the placing of *She's Leaving Home* has significance within the overall context of a concept album based on *alternative* life styles. *Fixing a Hole* explores personal freedom through psychedelic experience: *Being For the Benefit of Mr. Kite!* celebrates the camaraderie of a movement centred on love and togetherness.

> Outwardly by their appearance, inwardly by blasting their minds with drugs, rock and roll and communal sex; by abolishing families, nationalities, money and status, those of the new generation are disqualifying themselves from becoming somnambulating flunkeys of the power structure. The most intelligent of the young are dropping out.[43]

In contrast, the nameless suburban girl in *She's Leaving Home* opts out of one prescriptive environment for another.

The musical form of *She's Leaving Home* is both irregular and subtle. After a romantic four-bar harp introduction over a tonic E major triad, there is a five-bar vocal phrase which is extended by a lyrical three-bar cello counter-melody. The dramatic leap of a seventh (F#–E) is strongly reminiscent of *Eleanor Rigby* and the mood is heightened by the flattened seventh between the 2nd and 3rd bars of the verse (1st beat bar 2), a typical Beatles touch which adds to the sentimental 'period' flavour of the song.

Immediately a sense of relaxation is induced through the song's suggested association with an already familiar, patterned and in many ways pre-digested form, the waltz, and yet the underlying structure suggests off-balance apprehension. The next phrase of the tune appears regular and extends to four bars. However, what looks like a repeat of the four-bar phrase is extended to nine bars with a postlude this time of an inverted form of the counter-melody played by eight violins under the cello line. The verse section is completed by the two four-bar phrases to effect a continuous sense of narrative which is fed by Mike Leander's lushly romantic string arrangement. The effect is one of classic restraint which, if somewhat self-conscious, feeds the aural fabric to provide a clichéd yet powerfully haunting commentary on the lyrics.

The words, like the harmonies and beat, have a direct simplicity, yet this apparent naivety is deceptive. Suggestions of harmonic movement in the verse are frustrated by a constant reassertion of the tonic, and while it would be simplistic to suggest too strong a link with home-centredness in this harmonic structure, the avoidance of a dominant modulation does suggest fragile insecurity and a need for stability. The words support this interpretation, for the girl is leaving the security of home for a life organised around a faceless figure from the motor trade. Musically this is reflected in the lack of harmonic stability. The dominant ninth is unresolved and the listener is left with a comparable sense of insecurity.

The narrative continues: 'She's leaving home . . . after living alone for so many years . . .' against a falsetto parental vindication of their own position:

'We gave her everything money can buy . . . sacrificed most of our lives.' Again there is irregularity in the nineteen-bar chorus as the parents' vocal line overlaps with the continuing narration of the girl's story. Traditional urgency is encoded by heightened activity in the violins, and by the expectations generated by the extended passage of dominant sevenths of the dominant,[44] but the mood is deflated by the move to the subdominant A-major triad which then resolves plagally to E. A suggestion of resignation, an ironic 'so be it',[45] perhaps, to the whole somewhat pathetic tale. Certainly there is a sense of inactivity in the incantatory repetition of the parental commentary against the solitary 'She's leaving'. Yet the duetting has a mocking quality; there is an underlying sarcasm in the final punning 'bye-bye: buy buy' which heightens the contrast with the drifting melancholy of the waltz.

The problems expressed in *She's Leaving Home* are defined in relation to personal relationships. The simple narrative implies an almost casual, if whimsically tender, acceptance of life. In terms of social protest it questions the meaning of contemporary society, its foregrounding of 'everything money can buy' set against 'love' and the identity of the individual, but no solution is offered. Despite the final 'She's happy', the irregular structure and the constant denial of harmonic expectations suggest frustration. Here the use of the waltz form takes on added significance. Whereas *Sgt. Pepper's Lonely Hearts Club Band* juxtaposed the old with the new, *She's Leaving Home* is set entirely to a traditional form with its associations of the woman relying on the man's invitation to dance. Without it, she is the wallflower. The poignancy of the ballad lies in its musical setting, which forms a sad and sometimes ironic commentary on the failure of personal relationships in a conventional setting.

The first side of the album concludes with *Being for the Benefit of Mr. Kite!*, with its theatrical setting of fun, happiness and frivolity. Again there is a link with the LSD experience: 'The world becomes a circus, with the emphasis on parody – and our roles within it confirmed as clowns.'[46]

Being for the Benefit of Mr. Kite! has an immediacy of impact which is brought about by the directness of the narrative and the adoption of a carousel style. This has a twofold effect upon the listener. First it draws on popular memory and the psychological associations of the fairground to elicit a childlike response to a life promising non-stop amusement and pleasure. At this level the track suggests an anti-intellectual solution to the problems explored earlier of loneliness and alienation through a neo-proletarian sense of togetherness. At the same time the music provides a metaphor for the bond existing between performer and audience.

Again, there is a seeming nostalgia. The music draws on the rhythm of the carousel, regular but generator-powered as it pulses along. The melody line, while having a certain fairground tunefulness, is sufficiently repetitive to suggest a declamative announcement of events which are dramatically heightened by occasional syncopation, chromaticism and musical effects, although the voice itself is consistently deadpan and even ironic:

For the benefit of Mr. Kite
There will be a show tonight on trampoline. . .

Studio effects, including the use of a Hammond organ recorded at different speeds and overlaid with echo and four harmonicas, contribute to the fairground sound of the carousel. Antics on the trampoline are echoed in the falling sequences while the celebrated Mr. Kite performs his feat and Henry the Horse dances to the chromatic hurdy-gurdy waltz with its simple, vamped accompaniment. In this way, the timbres provide a non-verbal description of the lyrics' literal contents in evoking the sounds and performances of the fair.

There is a comparability to the opening track in the evocation of past and public show-biz. The fairground setting of *Mr. Kite* is a glitter with carousels, trapezes, men and horses, hoops and garters, a hogshead of real fire but it is just as much an affirmation of the buoyant mood of the Spontaneous Underground, which was held at the Marquee club in Wardour Street, Soho. Here there was a 'mixture of bands, poets, jugglers and all kinds of acts',[47] and 'Arthur Brown sang suspended, headgear aflame, swaying across the crowds in an eerie pendulum'.[48] While at surface level the fairground music evokes a proletarian 'night out' the mounting climax suggests otherwise. The increasingly lurching rhythms, the overlay of effects, the electronic manipulation of fairground sounds transform the musical structures, the chromatic runs of the hurdy-gurdy, to suggest hallucinogenic clowning, the 'throbbing psychedelics . . . the molten "high slides" and theatrical side shows'[49] of UFO and the Roundhouse. Within the total context of acid rock the showman, with his guarantee of a splendid time for all, calls up the image of Donovan's hurdy-gurdy man with his suggestion of drug-induced highs, 'bringing songs of love'.

While Harrison's *Within You Without You* seems at first to be a curious juxtaposition to *Mr. Kite*, as Neville points out

> although the contribution of marijuana to the evolvement of the New Man is marginal [compared with LSD], it is not irrelevant. It has broken down cultural/racial prejudice. Instead of being denigrated, African and Oriental lifestyles are now romanticised. It turns men into stoned Houdinis, who can escape the straitjacket of Aristotelian logic. Lateral thinkers, mystical drifters rarely maim other people.

> *Possible side effects*: A feeling of dreamy nonchalance, heightened sense of awareness, bursts of introspection, a mellowing attitude towards one's fellow man (especially if he's stoned beside you) and a formidable sense of contemporaneity.[50]

While the musical and lyrical codings of *With a Little Help from my friends, Lucy in the Sky with Diamonds, Getting Better, Fixing a Hole* and *Being for the Benefit of Mr. Kite!* evoke psychedelic experience, the raga motifs and use of tambouras, dilruba, tabla and sitar resonate both with the

beads, bells and joss sticks of the underground and with the India of the
Bhagavad Gita.

Within You Without You is the album's longest song and takes up many
of the themes explored on side one :

the space between us all
And the people – who
hide themselves behind a wall of illusion

The merging of the Beatles' familiar pentatonic/modal melodicism with the
Asian sound of the sitar can be interpreted as Harrison's solution to the
problem of loneliness established on the opening track of the album. As
Mellers points out, Harrison's playing of the sitar

doesn't rival or even seriously emulate, the 'real right thing', for the
orientalism is recreated in terms of the Beatles' newborn innocence . . . in
Harrison's song the freeing of the mind literally breaks the time-barrier,
so that the metres shift, over the endless drone, between fours, fives and
threes.[51]

The rocking fourths and flattened sevenths are similar to those in *Fixing a
Hole*, but here the freeing of the mind ('when you've seen beyond yourself
. . . the time will come when you see we're all one, and life flows on within
you and without you'), the chant-like singing, the endless drone suggest an
alternative and metaphysical way of life rather than one focused on LSD. It
is difficult to place the song outside of Harrison's personal search for
identity and meaning through Eastern mysticism.

'Acid', Harrison told the *Los Angeles Free Press* in August, [1967] 'is not
the answer, definitely not the answer. It's enabled people to see a little bit
more, but when you get really hip, you don't need it.' Later, to Hunter
Davies of the London *Sunday Times*, McCartney announced that they'd
given up drugs. 'It was an experience we went through and now it's over
we don't need it any more. We think we're finding other ways of getting
there.' In this effort they're apparently being helped by the Maharishi
Mahesh Yogi, the Indian founder of the International Meditation
Society, though even on the way to their initiation in Bangor, North
Wales, Lennon wondered if the experience wasn't simply going to be
another version of what they already knew: 'You know, like some are
EMI and some Decca, but it's still really records.'[52]

Lennon's cynicism seems to be reflected in the leery laugh with which the
song ends, a reminder, perhaps, that 'If religion is the opium of the people,
the Hindus have the inside dope'.[53] *Within You Without You* could suggest
a link with cannabis, used for centuries in India 'for its mind-altering effect,
being used primarily for religious and medical purposes. Hindus came to
speak of the drug as "the heavenly guide" and "the soother of grief".[54] The

laugh, like the 'hey hey hey' in *Fixing a Hole* may be yet another of Lennon's mocking asides.

Harrison's lyrics are explicit, however:

Try to realise it's all within yourself no-one else can make you change

Within the context of *life* itself the song has a direct bearing on *When I'm Sixty-Four*, a track which deals humorously with growing old in its identification of people who have come to terms with life at the most basic level of relationships with other 'lonely people'. 'One is free to love independently, to love everyone and also to experience love in a personal and intimate way. Love unites the world, but each person seeks his own meaning within it and within himself.'[55]

In their early music the Beatles had shown their ability to absorb different elements in current rock styles and make them work within their own music through witty and inventive commentary. Even as late as *Abbey Road* their music could be described as derivative in the most positive sense of the word and *When I'm Sixty-Four* evokes the twentyish music-hall style of George Formby in the shuffling syncopation of the introductory clarinet duet, the simple vocal melody, and the breaks in the accompaniment which reduce the texture to only bass and vocal soloist. The neatness of fit between lyrics and music suggest a world far removed from either metaphysical searching or hallucinogenics.[56]

Naive dreams, the 'cottage on the Isle of Wight' are gently mocked by a chorussed 'Oooo'. The down-to-earth rhyming incantation 'will you still need me, will you still feed me?' contrasts with the emphasis on love of the previous song, the people who 'never glimpse the truth – then it's far too late – when they pass away'. Here the truth lies in the jaunty description of chores. But it reflects a slightly nostalgic and sentimental past and the mockery is gentle:

You can knit a sweater by the fireside
Sunday morning go for a ride.

Verse three, in particular, with its 'Give me your answer, fill in a form' reads like a parody of the lonely hearts bureau, tying the song to the opening track, with its 'lonely people'. So while the cheerfulness of the tune persists, carrying with it the implication that on-the-surface solutions may be found in conventionalised relationships, the question remains, 'will you still need me, will you still feed me when I'm sixty-four ?'

Perhaps it is simply because there is none of the underlying self-searching of acid rock that *When I'm Sixty-Four* comes over as a simple 'it's all right with the world' song. Yet at the same time it is a protest against materialism, the world adults have made, and the song shows a child-like observation: mending a fuse, knitting by the fireside. It is 'disturbing as well as wistful'.[57]

There is a touching contrast between the first phrase, naively pentatonic despite the chromatic passing note, and the piquant rising and falling chromatics of the second phrase: while the middle section – minor thirds for the cottage in the Isle of Wight, sustained minims arching up to a high G for the recognition that 'you'll be older too' – underlines the pathos of the commonplace.[58]

'Digging the weeds' may reflect Lennon's punning humour with its passing reference to dope, but overall the *clichés*, bantering style, the 'ho's' and 'hums', the flippant 'oos', the tuba commentary gently poke fun at a past which is far removed from the search for positive regeneration inherent in *Within You Without You*. The general impression is one of gentle mocking and the 'neatness' of the final instrumental cadence ties up the ends, to suggest a conventional conclusion, one which contrasts with the gradual fade-out of the album's songs encoding psychedelic or metaphysical experience.

The apparent simplicity of *When I'm Sixty-Four* links the song to many of the early Beatles songs such as *She Loves You* or *I Saw Her Standing There*, which also reflect an uncomplicated and unsophisticated world. Within the context of the album, the significance of the song lies more in its identification of basic relationships with other lonely people. If *Nowhere Man*, *Eleanor Rigby* and *She's Leaving Home* comment on the loneliness of individuals trapped by an uncaring society, then *When I'm Sixty-Four* and *Lovely Rita* take a more pragmatic approach to life. The solution to problems, as demonstrated in the songs, is not through drugs or meditation, but through a comically casual and good-natured acceptance of life.

The links between *When I'm Sixty-Four*, *Lovely Rita* and the counter-culture appear tenuous. Seen in relation to the Beatles' own background there is a certain continuity. John Lennon's *A Spaniard in the Works* reflects a child's view of the world. 'Animals and freaks have comic dignity while adults look silly and too big, bending over and crawling. A double suggestion runs through the writing . . .: adults *are* silly . . . they talk jabberwocky about politics and color and religion and they believe what they say.'[59] *Nowhere Man*, *Paperback Writer* and *Penny Lane* similarly reflect on illusions and the sterile, ritualised roles of the adult world.

Further, while it could be argued that the counter-culture itself had a tendency to sexual stereotyping,[60] the women in *When I'm Sixty-Four* and *Lovely Rita* suggest an alignment with popularised mainstream culture, where they present no danger, no hidden meaning. The woman in *When I'm Sixty-Four* will blossom into the Old Dutch of the music hall, while Rita can simply be towed off for a session on the sofa. She is another spoof on romantic love, 'a whore in Liverpool, who procures through her daytime trade as a meter-maid'.[61]

The question arises of whether either song can be linked to the counter-culture either musically or culturally, or whether the Beatles' eclecticism and audience identification had led to their producing an album which was

capable at one level of 'internationalising the acid experience'.[62] By appeal-
ing to a mainstream audience, the Beatles had subtly introduced and
popularised aspects of a hippy-based ideology (love, drugs). The extent to
which this was recognised is difficult to ascertain, but nevertheless the fact
that they had gone 'hippy' ensured that many who would not consciously
identify with drugs, for example, took on the external signifiers (prayer
beads, paisley skirts, etc.). Equally, it could be argued that by popularising
and commercialising the hippy philosophy, they had contributed towards the softening of counter-cultural politics. Either way, it is suggested
that their songs 'don't lose the overall parameters of meaning which they
bring with them, but the precise meanings these take on in practice are
orientated through the effect of the new context in which they find
themselves'.[63]

The positioning of *When I'm Sixty-Four* and *Lovely Rita* provide some
indication of their significance on the album. Mellers suggests that in
following *Within You Without You* they indicate a rebirth, comparable to
that of *Tomorrow Never Knows* on *Revolver*.[64] But looking at the whole
album, one is forced to ask whether loneliness and alienation are so easily
overcome. Certainly it is no great surprise to find that the repeat of the *Sgt.
Pepper* chorus is no more than a false reprise/reprieve. Life is not really in
harmony and tensions are not so easily relieved. It is not straightforward
either to go back to an idealised past or to accept an oversimplified
celebration of the present.

When I'm Sixty-Four and *Lovely Rita* subtly attack the 'out there'. It is
possible to sing of a comfortable old age, of sex on the sofa, but these are no
more than escape mechanisms, a hark-back to the 'you've never had it so
good' ploy of the 1950s. The songs are further examples of the Beatles'
'creative questioning of life', an 'irreverant mockery of normal social
conventions'.[65] Viewed in the light of the counter-culture's attack on
spiritual emptiness and puritanical repressiveness, Lennon's *A Day in the
Life* can be the only real conclusion to the album. If there is no positive
communication between the world's lonely people, then the holocaust
ending of *A Day in the Life* may be the outcome.[66]

So the immediate surprise at the jaunty mood of *When I'm Sixty-Four*
and *Lovely Rita* is therefore justified, for their light hearted approach to life,
the flippant mood and emphasis on materialism, appears in many ways
inappropriate to an album exploring loneliness and the route to regeneration. *Getting Better* may have made use of a similar genre, *Being for the
Benefit of Mr. Kite!* may have evoked a mood of proletarian togetherness
through its carousel-like tunefulness, but *Within You Without You* had
prepared its audience for a process of spiritual rebirth.

The brisk, on-the-beat style of *Rita*, the regularity of the pulse, the
optimistic shape of the melody line all contribute to the image of the woman
herself, without complications and predictable. Aurally, the song bounces,
and with it Rita, 'sitting on the sofa with a sister or two'.

Rita's world is all-public. Her total personality is summed up in her description:

In a cap she looked much older,
And the bag across her shoulder
Made her look a little like a military man

which is fed by the bugle-like shape of the melody. This, in turn, contrasts with the pseudo-poetic opening ('Lovely Rita meter maid') to construct a hybrid image of the folk-lore maiden/call girl, milking the meters and 'filling in a ticket in her little white book'. The piano solo also mixes hybrid styles, blending barrelhouse and stride in a manner similar to that of *Good Day Sunshine* while the high-pitched, falling vocal 'oohs' in thirds have links with such early Beatles' numbers as *Thank You Girl*.

With Rita's role established at the onset, it is not surprising that the pulse is regular until the coda, when this regular beat is modified and transformed to match the sexual rhythmic panting set in motion by the 'nearly made it' of the preceding verse. Reality and fantasy appear to coincide with the rhythm following the sensuous panting while the car dubbing creates the double image of the traffic warden/prostitute.

In the following song, *Good Morning, Good Morning*, the jaunty opening, the crowing cockerel, the repeated 'Good morning' appear strangely in conflict with the previous two songs, although at one level there is a continuation of the fantasy/reality theme. The unchanging nature of urban life remains, but instead of Rita, barnyard noises effect an initial outlet. A strong rhythmic riff impels the melodic line forward reflecting the seeming urgency of non-stop movement downtown, while the repetitive narrow-ranged harmonies and phrases create the musical equivalent of the routine of city life: 'Nothing to say but what a day'.

In the second part of the song, Lennon and McCartney seem to comment from the outside on the universality of the experience: the day promises nothing, but around 'five o'clock . . . everyone you see is full of life'. This time the off-beat phrasing goes against the basic metronome beat of the alternating minims to create a curiously ambivalent feeling of timelessness which conveys both the deadening reality of daytime boredom and the optimism accompanying the end of routine work.

The subversion of the beat is also there in the changing time signatures, with the first eleven bars of the verse exhibiting changes of 5/4–3/4–4/4–5/4–4/4–3/4–4/4 in metre. The opening 5/4 section 'Nothing to do to save his life – call his wife in', whilst having a regularity of beat, has a curious syncopation which moves the important word stresses on. The 4/4 'everybody knows there's nothing doing . . .' uses off-beat phrasing to the same effect, while the 3/4 'I've got nothing to say but it's OK' contracts the opening 5/4 bars to push the piece onwards to the 4/4 'Good Morning'. At one level the song reflects the repetitive nature of life but the subversion of beat/time points towards psychedelic coding and it is not surprising that the final 'Good Morning, Good!' takes off in an unexpected direction. Dogs, cats, roosters, birds, the noise element itself, invades both the music and city life. There is a mysterious sense of compulsion in the repeated and exuberant 'Good Morning, Good!', a flight from reality into non-reality as the mundane is gradually transformed into the sensational.[67]

At this point *Good Morning* pre-empts the psychedelic coding of *A Day in the Life* in its contrast of everyday life with alternative experience. The barnyard invading the street is exciting, it allows for rejection of the ugly, the dull and the mundane as signified by the street noises; with the enveloping barnyard noise individual consciousness is opened out into a crazy larger-than-life world. According to Richard Neville: 'If Pavlov's dogs had taken LSD they would have danced to the sound of the bell, not salivated.'[68] The opening thus prefaces the psychedelic coding context of the whole piece. The cockerel stands for life, the rebirth of each day and within the context of acid rock, and in the final chorus, it is pulled into association with psychedelic flight where 'you will almost certainly come down safely . . . but not necessarily in the same spot you took off from'.[69]

In this way the *Sgt. Pepper* reprise is subtly changed. Ringo's 'hup two three four' sets a faster pace, the military band is on the retreat and the words reiterate 'Sergeant Pepper's Lonely' four times. The 'it's getting very near the end' suggests that there might be time for the traditional encore, but the fade-out to *A Day in the Life* with its gentle opening guitar chords is reflective rather than lively.

The song opens with softly strummed acoustic guitar chords and the verse describes a suicide with a conciseness comparable to that displayed in *Eleanor Rigby*: 'I read the news today, oh boy'. The mild interjection 'oh boy' is the first hint of disillusionment but seen in relation to the whole song, it appears yet another instance of Lennon's irony.

The song is built on a series of tense, reflective passages followed by soaring releases. The dispassionate account of events is reinforced by the simplicity of narration, both verbally and through the music. There is no extraneous detail, and the pentatonic melody follows the natural inflection of the words. The lack of modulation also works to make the imagery more powerful as it evokes the monotony of the continual newscasting and the reading of horrendous events which are passively consumed and passively forgotten. Conformity ('A crowd of people stood and stared', 'a crowd of people turned away') conjures up images of the amorphous mass, the mindless credulity of 'them'. Materialism is confronted by the headlines 'about a lucky man who made the grade' and the response, 'Well, I just had to laugh', links the song to *Within You Without You*, 'the people who gain the world and lose their soul'.

The out-there is then rejected: the refrain 'I'd love to turn you on' is paralleled by an electronic crescendo which suggests a drug-induced 'rush' and the audience is moved on to a differently coded, though thematically connected idea. While the first section explores the impersonal newsreading, the middle section, written by McCartney, has a stronger beat, a more urgent tempo:

Woke up, fell out of bed
Dragged a comb across my head . . .

There are comic pantings and realistic details: Found 'my coat and grabbed my hat, made the bus in seconds flat'. The music has a nervous dissonance as the percussive drumbeat melts into a panting chug but again there is a move towards psychedelic flight and release, 'Found my way upstairs and had a smoke, somebody spoke and I went into a dream'. Coming out of the trip is coded by the descending deep strings and two bars of unison brass. The original theme then returns along with the opening declaration: 'I read the news today oh boy'.

Psychedelic release is thus juxtaposed with the realities of everyday life. The equivocal 'four thousand holes in Blackburn, Lancashire' references 'either the police probes in the Moors murder case, or . . . a local councillor's complaints about the state of the roads'.[70] For another writer they represent the audience in the Albert Hall who, like the 'lovely audience, are only so many holes; unfilled and therefore unfertile holes . . . gathered together but separate and therefore countable, utterly and inarticulately alone'.[71]

The final 'I'd love to turn you on' leads directly into another electronic trip. This time the concentration of noise and distortion equates both with a symbolic romantic anarchy and with an hallucinogenic 'rush' of alarming intensity:

Come to the edge
We might fall
Come to the edge
It's too high
COME TO THE EDGE
and they came
and he pushed
and they flew . . .[72]

The explosive crescendo of *A Day in the Life* parallels, to some extent, Greil Marcus's definition of a *pop* explosion

that cuts across lines of class and race . . . and, most crucially, divides society itself by age. The surface of daily life (walk, talk, dress, symbolism, heroes, family affairs) is affected with such force that deep and substantive changes in the way people think and act take place. Pop explosions must link up with, and accelerate, broad shifts in sexual behaviour, economic aspirations, and political beliefs . . . [A pop explosion must be] capable of easy, instantaneous and varied imitation and extension, in a thousand ways at once: it must embody, suggest, affirm and legitimize new possibilities on all fronts even as it outstrips them.[73]

Returning to Tim Leary's view that the album 'gave voice to a feeling that the old ways were out . . . it came along at the right time that summer',[74] the question arises of the extent to which *Sgt. Pepper* was a 'breakthrough'. In America,

> the kids tried to identify with their heroes' music, just as they had done in the past, with the result that life began to imitate art. *Sgt. Pepper* broke with the convention, yet unwittingly established a convention of its own. Without knowing why, the great vacuous mass of America's teenagers decided it was supposed to have all these new things, with which the Beatles seemed to be involved. They wanted costumes, Salvation Army band coats, bells, beads, painted faces and all the other absurd paraphernalia. The average youngster in Des Moines saw a picture of John Lennon wearing flowered pants and immediately ran out and bought himself a pair . . . Left to their own devices, the Beatles had really triggered something.[75]

Within three months of its release, *Sgt. Pepper* attracted 2.5 million buyers.[76] In England there was a parallel response.

> The image of the Beatles has been projected into a whole canopy of activities – from the absurd SWINGING LONDON fiction to the cult of asinine whimsy that produced transcendental meditation for suburbia but, wide though their more serious social repercussions may have been, it has always remained their dazzlingly versatile music that has elevated them so far above the commonplace. The Beatles have often been associated with the progressive side of pop music, and for many they have been the standard-bearers into new dimensions of music.[77]

' "They're untouchable", said Cass Elliott of the Mamas and the Papas. "No matter how hard anybody tries", said one of our most successful young producers, "no matter how good they are, almost everything we do is a cop on the Beatles." '[78] Roger Waters considered *A Day in the Life* to be 'one of the greatest tracks ever made' and believed it vindicated the Floyd's decision to combine live performance with 'stuff . . . [that is] completely impossible to do live'.[79] Jagger was equally convinced that *Sgt. Pepper* showed the way forward. 'The Stones might speak to one's personal condition in a way that the Beatles did not, but the Beatles were universal.'[80] '*Sergeant Pepper's Lonely Hearts Club Band* . . . is traditionally regarded as the apex not only of their career, but of rock music *per se*.'[81]

While it could be argued that *Sgt. Pepper* simply brought together many of the ideas earlier explored by the Beatles in their investigation of loneliness and the psychedelic, there is nevertheless a sense of thematic development and structure which supports the notion of a concept. No longer a simple miscellany, the album is a sequence of intricately linked songs which are performed without a break.

At one level it explores 'the perennial as well as current problems of adolescence – loneliness, friendship, sex, the generation gap, alienation, fear, nightmare'.[82] As a concept, the narrative can support this interpretation. Structurally a unity is achieved by the opening theme and its later reprise, both stressing camaraderie, and by the lyric continuity which explores themes of separate loneliness and their possible solutions. Underlying the overall shape of the LP there is an arch form with *Within you Without You* constituting the thematic central point in its search for the self, drawing on the eastern

> heritage of gentle, tranquil, and thoroughly civilized contemplativeness. Here we have a tradition that calls radically into question the validity of the scientific world view, the supremacy of cerebral cognition, the value of technological prowess; but it does so in the most quiet and measured of tones; with humor, with tenderness, even with a deal of cunning argumentation. . . . However sternly one may wish to reject the world view of Lao-tzu, of the Buddha, of the Zen masters, one cannot fairly accuse such figures of lacking intellect, wit, or humane cultivation. . . . Though their minds lay at the service of a vision that is incompatible with our conventional science, such men are the prospective participants of neither a lynch mob nor a group-grope party. Fortunately, their example has not been lost on our dissenting young; indeed, it has become one of the strongest strains of the counter-culture.[83]

As such the mood of *A Day In the Life* is not as disjunct as it might at first appear. As an encore to the reprise, it finally takes on board the 'lonely people' and with 'wit, tenderness, cunning argumentation' and 'quiet and measured tones' calls into question the meaning of contemporary society. To ignore the vision is to invoke the consequence and the final instrumental crescendo paints a scenario of devastation that is balanced only by Lennon's invitation to psychedelic experience, 'I'd love to turn you on.'

> If we accept the proposition that the counter-culture is, essentially, an exploration of the politics of consciousness, then psychedelic experience falls into place as one, but only one, possible method of mounting that exploration. It becomes a limited chemical means to a greater psychic end, namely, the reformulation of the personality, upon which social ideology and culture generally are ultimately based.[84]

The connection between psychedelic experience and visionary religion thus falls into place and mystical experience and LSD are established as two complementary facets in the search for a new reality.[85] The opening chorus establishes the theme of the 'lonely hearts' and in *With a Little Help From My Friends* there is a juxtaposition of isolation and support which reinforces the need for 'knowledgable guidance' for the first-time user of

LSD. *Lucy* then transforms the experience of LSD into a musical form to provide both an equivalent intensification of subjective experience and a link with other psychedelic songs and posters of the same period. *Getting Better* focuses on knowledge ('you gave me the word') while *Fixing a Hole* carries the LSD experience one stage further. At this point the user is on his own, confident that 'Where I belong, I'm right'. *Being for the Benefit of Mr. Kite* again evokes psychedelic experience in the final mounting climax where the sound collage has a similarity of effect to that of the ending of *Good Morning. Within You Without You* is equivocal in meaning, drawing possibly on cannabis, but overall it is metaphysical in its vision and deterministic in its rejection of the egocentricity of western civilisation with its competitiveness, reserve and worldliness. Occupying a pivotal position on the record, it links with *A Day in the Life* which pulls on the relationship between drug experience and catharsis. All eight songs confront the problems of the outside world and propose and celebrate the counter-cultural alternative.

She's Leaving Home, *When I'm Sixty-Four* and *Lovely Rita* occupy the antithesis of the regenerative process. *She's Leaving Home* is an eloquently tender rejection of society. No solutions are offered to the problems raised, but clearly there is no need when the song is set within the overall context of the album. If the girl chooses to swap one negative life style for another, then that's her option, but the outcome can only be a fragile insecurity. The self-assurance found in the psychedelic songs is missing, to be replaced with a haunting image of loneliness which rebounds against the 'never had it so good' world of mainstream culture.

When I'm Sixty-Four and *Lovely Rita* are equally subversive in their subtle attack on the middle-class ploys of the dominant culture for the characters in both songs also subsist, albeit cheerfully, in the world identified in *Good Morning* and *A Day in the Life*.

> As such they provide insights rather than solutions to the problems of a society which revolves around materialism, repressive affluence and individual conformity.

The *Sgt. Pepper* reprise is no more than a formal requirement. It is the end of the show, but the final track is no jovial encore. Rather, it sums up the underlying message of the album. This time there is no characterisation, just an expression of Lennon and McCartney's personal realisation of the futility of the 'out-there' world: the juxtaposition of the inhumanity of the dominant culture with that of the counter-culture, the need to know oneself, to open up to alternative experience: 'I'd like to turn you on'.

4   1967 and Psychedelic Rock

Although it would be a sweeping generalisation to say that the British record charts of 1967 were totally dominated by flower power hits, there was nevertheless a strong move towards songs combining a heady infusion of love and acid. In January 1967 Donovan set the mood with *Sunshine Superman* which had moved up to No. 3 on the charts, and this was quickly followed up by *Mellow Yellow* and the Beatles' *Strawberry Fields Forever*, a key hallucinatory track. The Jimi Hendrix Experience released *Purple Haze* and *The Wind Cries Mary*; Procol Harum *A Whiter Shade of Pale* and the Kinks, *Waterloo Sunset*. July continued the trend, with Cream's release of *Strange Brew*, but by this time the emphasis was moving increasingly towards love and sentimentality, a possible reaction to an acid experience.[1] This was encapsulated by the Beatles' *All You Need Is Love* and the Stones' somewhat untypical *We Love You*. Of even greater significance was the release of the Beatles' pivotal concept album, *Sgt. Pepper's Lonely Hearts Club Band*, and its dark counterpart, the Stones' *Their Satanic Majesties Request*, both of which encoded the acid experience through multi-layered esoteric references.[2] At the same time, the West Coast scene moved into focus with Scott McKenzie's *San Francisco*, which was immediately followed up by the Flowerpot Men's *Let's Go to San Francisco*.[3]

In retrospect there was a certain inevitability about songs popularising psychedelic experience. As Joel Fort pointed out in 1969,

> Most young people are not manning the ramparts, fighting for social change and progress, but rather, like their elders, are apathetic, accepting or resigned to things as they are . . . Although the activists or so-called New Left [and New Right] receive considerable attention and are thought by many to represent American youth, they probably number no more than tens of thousands in such groups as the Students for a Democratic Society, (SDS), antiwar and antidraft groups, student power advocates and some elements of the hippies and Yippees. Then there are the equally radical groups of special minorities, namely the Black Panthers, Brown Berets, and others seeking power, dignity, and sometimes justice for

racial and cultural minorities. There is a much larger group of our young who . . . express their underlying discontent with the *status quo* by their involvement in folk-rock. American pop culture today is probably for the first time determined by youth who, with folk-rock, acid-rock, raga-rock, light shows, poster art and the psychedelic scene in general, have determined the cultural values for the society.[4]

In Britain there were even fewer songs which displayed a consciousness of political goals,[5] and overall the counter-culture was involved in 'cultural politics'; 'the fight was not on the level of the political system but that of personal freedom: the freedom to experience and enjoy'.[6] Their heroes, like those of their American counterparts, included Bob Dylan, the Byrds, Jefferson Airplane, the Mothers of Invention, the Doors, Cream, Pink Floyd, Jimi Hendrix, the Beatles and the Rolling Stones.

By 1967 many songs had emerged with drug themes: *Mr Tambourine Man, Eight Miles High, Mayrowana, Marijuana, Mother's Little Helper, Good Vibrations, Yellow Submarine, A Groovy Kind of Love* and *Sunshine Superman*.[7] The popularising of psychedelic music was largely due to the American record industry's realisation that 'groups with long hair, silly names, and no obvious hit singles in their repertoire had to be taken seriously'.[8] The open-air 'Be-In' festival in Golden Gate Park, San Francisco, had attracted 20,000 people and had featured such pioneering acid-rock groups as Country Joe and the Fish, Moby Grape, the Quick-silver Messenger Service, the Steve Miller Band, Jefferson Airplane and the Grateful Dead, all bands who had featured regularly on FM top forty radio.

> Pausing to take a drag on a joint between words, the announcers made it clear that they were part of the new subculture, and they helped to exaggerate some of the divisions in popular music between artists who were seen as being part of the traditional 'show business' sector of the music industry, and the hip alternative groups who were building a new future.[9]

> A dazed Santa Claus liberally threw LSD capsules and marijuana to the winds. An overawed *Time Magazine* recorded, 'The huge crowd was peaceful . . . an amazing tribute to Haight-Ashbury.' More accurately, it was a tribute to LSD which had begun to suppress local aggression on an ever-increasing scale.[10]

Although it has been argued that the Monterey Festival of June 1967 was 'a deliberate attempt by organisers Lou Adler and Alan Pariser to recreate the "Be-in" for the people of the record industry and the national media who had missed it the first time around',[11] there is little doubt that both its scale and wide coverage made it an event of supreme importance in the rock world. Hippie music had been seen to have distinct commercial possibilities: Jefferson Airplane had released their first album, *Takes Off*, and Adler and

Pariser were equally keen to promote other San Franciscan groups who had joined the San Fransiscan scene. American acts on the bill included the Byrds, the Paul Butterfield Band, the Grateful Dead, the Blues Project, the Mothers of Invention, Simon and Garfunkel and the Doors. Scott McKenzie joined with John Phillips and the band for a version of his hit single *San Francisco*, which had already sold over five million copies in the States alone. Paul McCartney, Donovan, Mick Jagger and Bob Dylan were on the Board of Directors and Brian Jones was there as guest MC. Cream, the Young Rascals, the Beach Boys and Lovin' Spoonful had also been invited.

Apart from setting a precedent for similar events in the States and in England the roots of Monterey – the free outdoor concerts and the non-profit, celebratory theme – were soon distorted as visions of large profits arose from the excitement over the commercial viability of the new music and the attendant paraphernalia of beads, bells, headbands and posters. Flowers, marijuana and LSD were in abundance and although the Festival was free from trouble, drug usage was quickly picked up on by politicians, editors, publishers and administrative bureaucrats as a subject which could easily be oversimplified and distorted. As Joel Fort points out,

> the more [drugs] are talked about and used to monopolize public attention, the less the candidate or office holder needs to talk about the real criminal, social and health problems of the society. Reality in effect is obscured by a cloud of smoke or hot air. Many other phenomena . . . are of course used, but none so consistently or so effectively as a few drugs such as marijuana, heroin, and LSD.[12]

Acid had been available in England since mid-1965, brought in by Michael Hollingshead from Tim Leary's Millbrook Centre, and by 1966 was used extensively at the Spontaneous Underground, at the Marquee. 'The invitation to the first afternoon read: "Who will be there? Poets, pop-singers, hoods, Americans, homosexuals (because they make up 10% of the population), 20 clowns, jazz musicians, 'one murderer', sculptors, politicians, and some girls who defy description are among the invited.' "[13] In general, nothing was promised, nothing advertised, nothing expected. Pink Floyd, as the resident band, performed against a backdrop of red and blue flickering lights while the dancers 'began that snakey undulating swaying associated with large amounts of acid, a triumph of chromosome-damaged cunning'.[14] 'If drugs are to be taken into account in the assessment of UFO it was perfectly obvious that LSD and pot created an atmosphere of harmony and inventiveness' and the 'fad for freakouts on a San Francisco scale spread through 1967'.[15]

Contemporary British reinforcement of the US psychedelic scene emerged in such slogans as 'Haight is love', 'Make Love Not War'. UFO was quickly headlined as London's answer to Haight-Ashbury; the Electric Garden, later renamed Middle Earth, opened in Covent Garden. Arts labs, local underground magazines, legalise pot rallies, free pop concerts and psychedelic shops provided evidence of the evolving counter community which, in the summer of 1967, seemed to be symbolised by flowers and songs celebrating the acid experience.

> The national press were quick to move in, the *People* and the *News of the World* . . . bandying around the Castalia Foundation's term 'psychedelic' like any popularised psychoanalytic phrase, talking about flower-power and drug crazed youths with that menopausal tone of total scandal that is guaranteed to bring the English clustering like flies to the subject as participants or sight-seers. Nine months after the first gatherings in Haight Ashbury mill-girls and office workers were wandering down the Brighton and Blackpool seafronts, jangling their souvenir prayer-belts, trailing their paisley bedspreads, brandishing daffodils and trying to look tripped out. The Beatles had gone 'flower power' and it was up to the kids to do their best to follow.[16]

In retrospect the summer of 1967 can be seen as a turning point in the British counter-culture as it was then that it attracted thousands of adherents and sympathisers. Yet it is very doubtful whether this rapid conversion involved either personal experience of LSD or a commitment to the political aims of the movement. As Tom McGrath wrote before leaving the *International Times*:

> this is not a movement of protest but one of celebration . . . those involved in the 'new thing' are having a good time now. And they are succeeding. This gives rise to envy and creates enemies. Favourite put-downs against the new movement are 'frivolous' and 'irresponsible.' The 'pleasure now' attitude ensures, however, that whatever happens, this is one revolutionary movement that must win one way or another. . . . Even to call it a new 'movement' is to create a false impression. This new thing is just people coming together and grooving. If you don't know what grooving means then you haven't yet understood what is going on. . . . There are influences ranging from the Beatles to William Burroughs. Leaders of comparable movements in the States don't have much of an influence here despite so many sneers to the contrary. . . . This movement is essentially optimistic. It has a happy view of man and his potential, based mainly on his creativity . . . The big world problems that concerned CND and the Committee of 100 at their zenith have not been forgotten. The new approach is to make positive changes wherever you are, right in front of your nose. The weapons are love and creativity – wild new clothes, fashions, strange new music sounds . . . The new movement is slowly, carelessly, constructing an alternative society. . . . It operates on different conceptions of time and space. The world of the future may have no clocks.[17]

The songs matched and contributed towards the mood of 1967, the unusually hot summer, the emphasis on love, on being 'beautiful' and 'doing your own thing'. Yet for the progressive rock musicians, the commercialisation of flower power had little in common with the reality of the underground, which continued to push towards an uncompromised experiential alternative. The soft-edged romanticism which characterised many of the songs of 1967 was too ephemeral to have any lasting effect on the direction of rock generally. By the autumn of '67 such groups as Cream, Pink Floyd and the Jimi Hendrix Experience focused increasingly on developing a music which was, above all, uncompromising in its originality and creativity while the Beatles and the Stones moved towards a more aggressive position with the release of *Lady Madonna* and *Jumping Jack Flash* respectively. Even so, the harassment of the Beatles and the Stones over drug charges, the focus on acid and 'free love' and the recognition generally that rock had grown up and was capable of presenting a strong anti-establishment challenge was significant. As Melly points out: 'there was no danger after that summer of pop becoming officially acceptable. It was tolerated, but only just. . .'. By the autumn, 'the Underground was no longer the property of a tiny minority. It had thousands of adherents and sympathisers, its own slang, its own meeting-places, its own heroes and more relevant here, its own groups.' [18]

Whilst *Sgt. Pepper* can be considered the key album of 1967, *Strawberry Fields Forever* ushered in acid rock. It was the Beatles' second psychedelic single. *Tomorrow Never Knows* had come out in 1966 and the lyrics were overtly drug-centred:

Turn off your mind, relax and float downstream. . .
Surrender to the void. . .
Listen to the colour of your dreams. . .

However, both musically and lyrically, *Tomorrow Never Knows* reads like a first attempt when compared with *Strawberry Fields Forever*. Both songs have a similar phrase shape and make use of the flattened seventh, both follow the irregular accenting of the words, but in *Strawberry Fields* the relaxed effect is intensified by stretching the eight-bar structure to nine:

Let me take you down . . . Strawberry Fields forever.

This subtle change in phrase length creates a laid-back mood, and as Lennon sings 'Strawberry Fields' for the first time the melody comes to rest on the flattened seventh to create a sense of the unpredictable. With the words 'Nothing is real' the tonality is further clouded by a variant of the earlier triplet motif which clashes against an unexpected VIb7 chord before coming to rest on the seventh. The subtlety of the underlying chord structure feeds the mood of changed consciousness. The shifting harmonies work against a sense of known direction to provide, instead, a dreamy feeling of vagueness. At the same time, there is a sense of reassurance. 'And nothing to get hung about' has a rapid IV–V–VI chord progression which moves finally towards a traditional V–I cadence on 'Strawberry Fields forever' – a sense of having arrived. This, in turn, feeds a subconscious response to a known harmonic progression, but one which, in the context of a song encoding hallucinogenics suggests an alternative sense of closure.

The LSD coding is particularly strong here. The effects of acid are unpredictable, and an experienced user is needed to take over and lead the initiate through what can often be a disturbing change in consciousness.[19] The Beatles' use of the familiar V–I cadence within an otherwise unpredictable chord structuring can be read as an expression of their own confidence: they have taken acid, know its effects and are capable and confident of taking the initiate through to *Strawberry Fields* where new perceptual, cognitive and affective sensations will be enjoyed.[20]

The shape of the melody is equally relaxed as it responds to the connotations of the words – the falling shape on 'Let me take you down', the displaced accent on 'to' subtly encoding a pause, a change in direction before the sensual imagery of *Strawberry Fields* is released into the consciousness.

In the second section of the song, the downward movement is maintained. The chords in the first four bars are based harmonically on the descending chromatic counter-melody first heard in the introduction. There is the suggestion of a musical metaphor for psychedelic experience as the music provides a route downwards into the subconscious. In this section in particular, perceptual changes are foregrounded, the imagery is strongly supported by the musical effects – the gentle pace, timbre, shifting chord structures, electronic distortion – to provide a seductive route to changed forms of consciousness. As if to emphasise the changing perceptions, each series of refrain–verse sections has its own unique texture and musical colouring.

The collage in the coda is especially strong in psychedelic references. A fragmentary and distorted guitar solo and repeated piano chords jar tonally with the cello line and indistinct cries. The mix fades in and out as flutes enter with a new motif which is out of tempo with the guitar, piano and percussion that follow. Finally the table harp reappears while a tape-manipulated voice is heard distantly intoning 'cranberry sauce'. The drum track fades and the song dies away, implying a distinct change in consciousness. Conventional sounds are subtly changed, there are strange mixtures of colour and texture. 'Follow this through to its logical conclusion – take acid – have an authentic experience and with our guidance you, too, can live in *Strawberry Fields Forever*.'

As an early psychedelic track, *Strawberry Fields Forever* was powerfully persuasive in evoking the colour and beauty of a trip. It emphasises enhancement of awareness, the positive side of consciousness expansion; any potentially disturbing aspects are left out. At the same time it implies that each LSD experience, like each user, is personal and unique[21] – 'No one I think is in my tree.' The overall mood of *Strawberry Fields Forever* is reassuring. So the acid experience is shown to be kaleidoscopic (musically encoded through the changes of tone, colour and texture) and gentle, 'easy with eyes closed, misunderstanding all you see'.

Even so, as Melly points out, the song demanded at least some knowledge of LSD.

> I didn't understand it at the time. I thought it was very beautiful, extraordinarily beautiful, but it made me feel like Alice looking through the little door in the wainscot at the garden beyond. In the event I was right to feel like Alice – there was indeed a little cake on the glass top table, or to be more exact, a sugar lump impregnated with LSD.[22]

While the Beatles pointed the way through *Tomorrow Never Knows* and *Strawberry Fields Forever*, Donovan can still be considered the guru of English flower power music. Under pop-impresario/producer Mickie Most, Donovan

> produced a series of quasi psychedelic, semi-classic singles, *Sunshine Superman*, *Mellow Yellow* and *There is a Mountain* through 1966–67. His third album, *Sunshine Superman* (1967) produced by Most and John Cameron, became something of an early acid-head bible. Then came the double set *A Gift From a Flower to a Garden* (1968) with its cover pin-up of guru Maharishi Yogi and flower power trimmings, which with *Sgt. Pepper* summed up that particularly whimsical period of pop 'progression'.[23]

As early as 1965, Donovan's songs hinted at the acid experience:

When I'm feeling spaced out
my sunshine comes out,
you just don't know what I mean,
Mmm, that's fine;

(*You Just Gotta Know My Mind*, 1965)

There are early references to marijuana, acid and other drugs,[24] but while there is a certain comparability with other drug songs of the period – Lovin' Spoonful's *Do You Believe in Magic*, the Mamas and Papas' *California Dreamin'* and Dylan's *Mr. Tambourine Man* – Donovan's songs show an extreme naivety. His guitar may have borne the logo 'This machine kills', but unlike Guthrie, he failed to stipulate what – 'This Guitar Kills Fascists' – and for many Donovan appeared at the time to be like an 'updating of one of those sentimental heroes in Dostoyevksy – Aloysha or Prince Myshkin, The Holy Fools. Innocence and Sweetness.'[25] Despite this, his songs showed a sensitivity to the mood of the moment: 'When you've made your mind up forever to be mine. I'll pick up your hand and slowly blow your little mind.'

Sunshine Superman creates an almost mesmeric effect through the underlying circular movement of the basic vocal riff and, with the exception of the A7 chord at the beginning of the chorus, the whole song is based on two slowly alternating chords, D7–G. The effect of these alternating harmonies with the movement of the melody line is one of a gentle circularity. As both chords are stressed equally neither has the reassuringly supportive effect of the tonic, and so a different tonal space is caused. Both chords have an equal pull on the melody line and create an effect of anti-gravity, drifting and timelessness: you only know where you are because of where you started. This timelessness is stressed by the use of rests which deflect the emphasis from the first beat of the bar. Along with the vaguely oriental sound of the 'twanging rhythm guitar and the plangent sustained quality of the lead guitar and the quasi-hallucinatory timbres' there is the suggestion of a 'mystical or trance-like experience'.[26] This is underlined by the title itself – *Sunshine Superman*. Again there is an emphasis on experience and/or knowledge.

> Sunshine is pure acid. A small piece will get you spaced . . . If you are dealing with sunshine, you know that you have a lot of power in your hands with an enormous responsibility for many heads. It's not dealing in the sense of making money. It's much closer to distributing sunshine . . . The aim of . . . L.S.D. basically is to get high, that is to expand the consciousness and find ecstasy and revelation within.[27]

The instrumental break starts with the basic riff shape of the verse form, and then moves quickly towards positive assertion by progressing directly to the chorus with its more traditional use of V–I harmony. The effect is similar to that of *Lucy in the Sky with Diamonds* and *Strawberry Fields Forever*.[28] There is an affirmative sense of movement traditionally associated with the cadential chord progression to confirm Donovan's ability as 'Sunshine Superman' to give the 'listener' a *beautiful* experience:

> you can sit there a-thinking
> On your velvet throne
> Down on a rainbow so you can
> Have all your own . . .

Mellow Yellow, released in 1966, entered the charts at No. 34 in February 1967 and rose to No. 8 in March. Its mood of gentle ease is established in the pacing of the vocal and general simplicity of musical texture in the opening phrases.

> I'm just mad about Saffron
> Saffron's mad about me

At the onset the song could be yet another love song, similar in many ways to Donovan's *Jennifer Juniper* in its gentleness. But the assertive 'Electrical banana', and self-nominated 'They call me Mellow Yellow' with its 'Quite rightly' aside leaves little doubt that the song is promoting the latest hallucinogen. Accidentals colour and highlight the 'Electrical banana' while the instrumental break builds on the melody line of the verse and moves to an assertive reiteration of the 'mellow yellow' motif. The overall effect, like that of *Sunshine Superman,* is mesmeric: the combination of repetition, bright timbres and the emphasis on being 'high' ('Born high forever to fly, wind velocity nil') feed the psychedelic message of the song. 'They call me Mellow Yellow "Quite Rightly" . . . If you want your cup I will fill.'

Again the connotations depended on 'being in the know'. Mellow yellow suggests the Acapulco gold type of marijuana, which can produce hallucinogenic effects, while the 'Electrical banana' which 'is bound to be the very next phase' is specific to the events of 1966 when

> there was a rumour that the dry scrapings from the inside of banana peel could have the same effect as LSD. This had originated from a theatre of the absurd play performed by a few hippies and reported by the underground press. Within days 'bananadrine', or as Donovan had called it 'Mellow Yellow' was being prepared and smoked by thousands, widely written up in the mass media, investigated by narcotics policemen and denounced by politicians. In the San Francisco area I saw those who had smoked innumerable cigarettes made from banana scrapings in hopes of getting high, but instead, getting sore throats and irritated lungs. The substance was even available by mail for five dollars a half ounce and could be purchased in stores for approximately a quarter of a cigarette. Government and private research grants were sought and obtained to study the pharmacology and sociology of this phenomenon, and one such report actually was published in the *American Journal of Psychiatry* in 1967.[29]

The Move's *I Can Hear the Grass Grow,* which is explicit in its focus on drugs, moved quickly to No. 5 in May 1967. Within the underground, however, the Move's 'overnight conversion to hippiedom' was regarded as 'hypocritical. . . . The point is that psychedelic music grew from an environment, a very specific London one. . . . It was anarchic, innocent and didn't really take itself too seriously.'[30] Roy Wood was regarded as 'a clever song-writer' with an ability 'to mould his own niche' and *I Can Hear the Grass Grow* was seen as an attempt to 'capture the essence of psychedelia and the swinging London underground of 1967'.[31] Even so, the song demonstrates a sensitive awareness of the potentially disruptive side effects of acid and the 'I need you to help now baby, Get a hold of yourself now baby' focuses on anxiety and the need for support.

The verses clearly describe an LSD experience:

> My head's attracted to a magnetic wave of sound
> With the streams of coloured circles
> making their way around. . .

There is a hazy underlying dissonance between the Eb support chord and the melody line, a sensation of drifting in the deflection of accents from strong to weak beats. The chorus moves to a more metrical beat, as if to affirm the synaesthetic effects of acid:

I can hear the grass grow
I see rainbows in the evening

with the lead break meandering raga-like around the Bb to suggest the trance-like state of both psychedelic experience and Indian mysticism. This emphasis on rhythmic, rather than harmonic constructional principles provides the timelessness associated with acid rock and correlates with the emphasis on escapism from the rational time sense.

However, while *I Can Hear the Grass Grow* pulled strongly on the musical characteristics of the counter-culture in its use of multiple coding in the musical styles and overtly psychedelic lyrics, the song is almost too slick and shows parallels with the Rolling Stones' *Their Satanic Majesties Request*. As an r&b band, the Move could have extracted ideas from their original style to produce new and individualised statements and musical relationships instead of this simple adoption of the musical characteristics of psychedelic rock.

While the Move were regarded with suspicion by the underground, the newly formed Procol Harum were sufficiently adventurous in musical style to attract a strong following at UFO. Their début single, *A Whiter Shade of Pale*, topped the British singles charts for six weeks in June and July 1967, breaking all kinds of records for copies sold each day. It remained in the top twenty for three months all but a week.

A Whiter Shade of Pale was very much of its time[32] in its evocation of surrealism and timelessness.[33] Musically, this is constructed through the transformation of Bach's *Sleepers Wake* chorale, with its spacious tempo and use of ritornello and ostinato. Only the musical construction of the chorale remains, yet the original words of the opening chorus can be heard in the mind

Sleepers Wake for night is flying
The Watchmen on the Heights are crying
Awake Ye Virgins
Night is past

to be subtly transformed by the new contextualisation: with LSD there can be a new life: 'thoughts which are ordinarily suppressed or repressed from consciousness come into focus and previously unseen relationships or combinations between them [are] recognised'.[34] With its reference to 'sixteen vestal virgins' and reinforced by a general feeling of the archaic 'the miller told his tale', the song combines hallucinogenic experience and tradition with a personalised vision of 'what could be'. There is a dreamy intensity, an evocation of an hallucinatory state which 'must have orchestrated a million trips'.[35]

The essence of the song is contained in the harmonic sequence which appears eleven times in all, plus a fade at the end. It appears initially in the instrumental introduction and is then used as the foundation for the two choruses, in which it is heard eight times in all. It also occurs in the two instrumental interludes. As such, it provides the total structure for the composition and while the chord sequence itself is complex, the use of the descending walking bass provides a sense of reassurance which, with the descending scale patterns is sufficiently memorable to provide an underlying feeling of stability.

The chord structure is particularly interesting, for whilst the use of the walking bass and the repetitious shifting harmonies work towards a timelessness, which is enhanced by the gradual fade-out, they have a similar effect to that of Fleetwood Mac's two-chord sequence (F7–G) in *Dreams*. Both create tonal space: in *Dreams* the anti-gravity is caused by each chord exerting an equal pull, which negates any move towards completion.[36] In *A Whiter Shade of Pale*, the movement towards a trance-like inevitability caused by the complex chain of chords and the walking bass supports the sustained and sensuous timbre of the vocal line which is made up of pentatonic falling shapes. These work independently of the rhythmic bass to create a further sense of freedom and floating, which is enhanced by the use of melisma at the end of the phrases.[37]

Whilst the lyrics suggest both the hallucinogenic:

The room was humming harder
As the ceiling flew away

and magic, in the reference to the Tarot cards,

But I wandered through my playing cards
And would not let her be
One of sixteen vestal virgins

the juxtaposition of images is far more important than is evident from line-by-line deconstruction. In combination with the haunting quality of the voice and the drift of the melodic shape, they give a general impression of heightened consciousness. Images collide and gently bounce off, their unlikely associations creating a new reality. The gentle pace of the song is also important in creating a feeling of space and time to enjoy the new experiences.

As Joel Fort comments:

This sometime enhancement of awareness or sensitivity and new synthesis of ideas are the . . . main basis for the religious-mystical or 'consciousness expansion' experiences that have been reported by some . . . and sometimes intense pleasurable or esthetic experiences [occur], such as a marked enhancement of a piece of music.[38]

The cumulative effect of the Bach chorale with its religious aura and the psychedelic imagery resonates with the counter-culture's 'rediscovery' of mysticism through hallucinatory experience:

> To see a World in a Grain of Sand
>   And a Heaven in a Wild Flower,
> Hold Infinity in the palm of your hand
>   And Eternity in an hour.
>
> (William Blake, Auguries of Innocence)

Procol Harum were not unique in making use of Bach. The Nice, also a psychedelic band, with keyboard virtuoso Keith Emerson, created orchestral settings of a souped-up Bach with jazzy improvisations and extensive tubular bells in *Brandenburger*. The delicate scoring of the Pentangle also made wide use of Baroque techniques and their repertoire included Italian medieval lyrics, Tallis's *Laments* and John Dowland's *Melancholy Galliard*. Like A *Whiter Shade of Pale* their music had an impeccable quiet in its harmonic treatment of rock.

While Jimi Hendrix is probably best known for the raw power of his guitar technique, *The Wind Cries Mary* is gentle. The haunting guitar motif which opens the song has an echo effect which resonates with the evocative 'and the wind whispers/cries/screams/Mary' to create an innate understanding. While *Purple Haze* evokes a powerful acid experience,[39] *Mary* is a much milder drug,[40] and the softer pacing of the song elicits a sense of complicity between Hendrix and the audience. There is muted understatement. Hendrix's voice, in particular, is at its most evocative, the words are spoken rather than sung out, with an off-the-beat inflection against a gently moving melody to create a mood of serenity and well-being that accompanies shared 'smoke.'

The basic chord structure is simple, moving through a repetitive C:Bb:F until the evocative:

> Footprints dressed in red
> And the wind whispers Mary. . .

Here the move to G7 followed by Bb has an underlying darkness, immediately counteracted by the brighter sound of the lead break which moves upwards in fourths with a gentle bending of slide notes to effect a musical equivalent of floating. There is an ease in tension on the penultimate note, a sudden stillness before the haunting lyrics of the last verse:

> Will the wind ever remember
> The names it has blown in the past

'And the wind cries Mary' is then picked up by the guitar motif, which gently bends the last note.

The Wind Cries Mary encodes the effect of marijuana through the gentleness and inner-directedness of its style. The timing is subtle, with the inflections in the melody line meandering just off the beat. The wind can blow anywhere, and the marijuana experience is universal.[41]

Whilst *The Wind Cries Mary* echoed the wider ethos of the underground, the Kinks' *Waterloo Sunset* focused on London, where the summer was moving fast into flower power. The song celebrates the love story of Terry and Julie in London's Waterloo. The song has an easy up-beat tempo, the lead guitar establishing the theme in the opening bars.

Overall there is a comforting sense in the repetitive nature of the song. Its underlying theme is the constant buzz of life in contrast to the quiet certainty of the 'dirty old river [that's] got to keep rolling, rolling into the night', and the sunset which unites everyone at Waterloo in a state of 'paradise'.

The lyrics present a nostalgic view of an unattractive environment: council flats, the underground station and the 'dirty old river'. In this it is linked to psychedelic tripping, when 'there is an enhancement of awareness or sensitivity which can focus on a love relationship. The experience can be intense and perceptual changes are mainly visual.'[42] While there is little in the music to suggest psychedelic coding,[43] the transformation of Waterloo into a rose-tinted paradise does suggest the influence of consciousness-expanding drugs, but as Neville points out, in the summer of 1967 'all the relevant sounds seemed somehow associated with acid and universal love'.[44] The focus on the positive aspects of *sunset* is interesting and there are possible connections with sunshine 'pure' acid: 'As long as I gaze on Waterloo Sunset, I am in paradise'.

While the Kinks had been on the best-selling artists list from 1964 to 1966, Pink Floyd were essentially an underground band. *Arnold Layne*, which had a short life in the top twenty, was adopted as one of the anthems of the underground, suggesting a certain exclusivity. It is probable that the lyrics were composed by Barrett while under the influence of LSD and the song cannot be divorced from UFO itself. As Miles points out: 'unlike the deadly seriousness of their American counterparts, the British groups turned out such classics as Arthur Brown's *Give 'im a Flower* and Smoke's *My Friend Jack Eats Sugar Lumps* and were always writing songs about dwarfs, gnomes and scarecrows.'[45]

At the time of its release Pink Floyd had turned professional and had made their first appearance on BBC-TV's 'Top of the Pops'. On May 12 they presented *Games for May* at the Queen Elizabeth Hall, London. The event was intended as a musical and visual exploration. The room was filled with millions of bubbles, there were moving liquid lights, 35mm film projections and the Floyd's road manager, dressed as an admiral of the fleet, threw huge bunches of daffodils to the audience. Barrett wrote new material, including *Games for May* which was issued as a single under its new title *See Emily Play* in June 'after days of messing about at EMI trying to repeat the sound they got with Joe Boyd on *Arnold Layne*'.[46] The group appeared three times on 'Top of the Pops' to promote *See Emily Play*; the song entered the charts in July and stayed there for seven weeks, reaching No. 9.[47]

See Emily Play gently hits at the girl who's 'often inclined to borrow somebody's dreams until tomorrow'. The main constructional principle is rhythmic, with the melody line supporting the off-beat, free-form poetry by the use of changing time signatures. There are somewhat cynical asides (A-hah) which comment on 'Emily [who] tries but misunderstands' and which suggest Barrett's personal response to those visitors to UFO and the Roundhouse who 'tripped out' on harmless sugar lumps, 'using them as an excuse to let go'.[48] But the words of the second and third verse are ambiguous. LSD can cause depression and suicidal thoughts and the Ophelia-like imagery

> Put on a gown that touches the ground
> (Ah-hah)
> Float on a river for ever and ever

does suggest a darker interpretation of the 'games for May' and the disorientating effects of hallucinogenic experience.

The chorus is more assertive with Barrett in the role of experienced user describing the effects of acid ('lose your mind') and linking this to the British underground's emphasis on play.[49] The quaver movement gives a strong sense of progress towards the jubilant 'Free' before the upward hallucinogenic flight suggested by the instrumental solo.

The song ends with a gradual fade-out over a I–V cadence. As it starts on the tonic chord over a strongly repeated key note, the final cadence suggests both a lack of finality and a sense of coming down in a different place.[50] This sense of incompletion feeds the ambiguity prevalent throughout the song and emphasises, in its lack of harmonic rationality, the hippy's characteristic dislike of logocentric meaning.

Like Floyd, Cream were against the singles market and while they had two hits in 1967 (*I Feel Free* and *Strange Brew*) they, too, moved increasingly towards albums which allowed for lengthy improvisation and a freedom of expression which could not be contained within the space of two or three minutes.

Strange Brew/Tales of Brave Ulysses had been released in June as a promotional single for their album *Disraeli Gears*. Accompanied by a 'Top of the Pops' promotion it reached No. 17 in the charts in July, with the album itself reaching No. 5.[51] Co-written by Clapton, Felix Pappalardi and his wife Gail Collins, *Strange Brew* set the tone for Clapton's playing on *Disraeli Gears* and has certain similarities with Hendrix in the use of electronic guitar effects such as fuzz tone, reverb and the wah-wah pedal, and in the psychedelic language both of the lyrics and of the sound itself.

Initially *Strange Brew* comes over as a heavy blues composition.[52] Bruce's bass riff supports the descending lead motif with its poised elegance, the bent notes accentuating the shaping of the line. The traditional blues focus on 'woman trouble' is supported by the 'woman tone' in the lead guitar. The repetitive line shape and the continuous bass riff work towards a feeling of fixation, of being taken over by the 'witch in electric blue'.

The sinuous lead guitar line, the distortion of the bent notes and resultant partials which hover around the melody line also move towards a sense of fixation, the sounds bending to the inflection of the words:

She's a witch of trouble in electric blue
In her own mad mind she's in love with you

In the chorus, the sense of the demon woman is opened out by the emphasis on the 'strange brew', the repetition moving towards an alternative fixation which is equally fatal, 'killing what's inside of you'. Overall, the song has an edginess possibly caused by incorporating electronic distortion into an otherwise classically restrained blues style. With the strong dip shapes on 'strange brew' and the repetitive riff it suggests a mood of obsessiveness and a possible mirroring of psychedelic experience. The image of the 'witch in electric blue' evokes the synaesthetic effects of LSD whereby one hears something seen, tastes something touched, sees something tasted. There is a sense of disorganisation too: 'On a boat in the middle of a raging sea she would make a scene' and addiction as the stress on physical dependence is pulled into association with the traditional blues alliance of 'woman trouble' and satanic imagery: 'If you don't watch out, she'll stick to you. Strange brew, killing what's inside of you.'

While singles provided particular insights into psychedelic experience, there is little doubt that the most influential record of the year was *Sgt. Pepper*, which was released on June 1, 1967 in the UK and a day later in the US. The album, which had taken four months to complete, was 'the grand overture to the summer of flowers and love. The Beatles' consummate interest in drugs and psychedelic fashion was being offered to the world.' [53]

Initially *All You Need Is Love* appears somewhat of a trite follow-up. 'In the words of Paoli Lionni "Love need not remain a banal cliché, but is and must be a constantly original and divine word." ' [54] So the repetitive 'Love, love, love' appears somewhat mundane, a soft-centred sing-along with little resemblance to the more aggressive connotations of love as an underground *weapon*.

However, given Lennon's innate sense of parody, a closer analysis suggests that the song takes on board many of the themes of 1967 in its popularisation of love and acid. There are fragments of old love songs and the inclusion of the opening bars of the French National Anthem reads like a tongue-in-cheek recognition that critics generally had hailed the *Sgt. Pepper* album as unifying 'the irreparably fragmented consciousness of the West, at least in the minds of the young'. [55]

Based on a recurring melodic motif, against a duetted 'love', the vocal is fronted to suggest a personalised statement 'that love is an all-pervasive and special force in the world, possibly an ultimate force'. [56]

Love, love, love
There's nothing you can do that can't be done. . .

The apparent sentimentality is then undercut by the 'altogether now' of the chorus with its passing reference to *Yellow Submarine*, a song which, with its acid connotations, had become somewhat of an anthem for the counterculture. Focused by this reference the song moves to its climax, which relates to the dangerous ecstasy of the acid experience.

The overlay of effects resemble the mood of the coda in *Being for the Benefit of Mr. Kite!* [57] and evokes both buoyant optimism and kaleidoscopic flashback. [58] There is a sense of compulsion in the repeated 'Love is all you need' which is heightened by the cheers and whistles of the 'audience'. The coding is psychedelic: LSD can lead to strong emotional bonds, positive feelings and alterations in the perception of time. Passing references to the Beatles' own songs, and to *Greensleeves* and the 1930s *In the Mood* are given a new perspective as they swing in and out of focus under the constant 'Love is all you need.' Released in summer 1967, the song seems to epitomise the love ethic which had characterised a generation's over-enthusiastic response to its own sense of collective identity. Yet the extended coda, with its faint echo of the refrain of *She Loves You*, suggests that the song may itself be a cynical comment on the so-called 'love' generation. By August, *All You Need Is Love* had moved to No. 1 in the British pop charts. At No. 21 was the Stones' *We Love You*. [59]

The difference between the Rolling Stones and the Beatles had involved both public image and music. 'Step-by-step, blow-by-blow, they followed each move of the Beatles with a complementary response: hard, heavy and dark, where the Beatles were soft and light.' [60] The release of *Their Satanic Majesties Request* and the single, *We Love You* seemed, then, to indicate a loss of direction. Despite the thrusting drive of the piano accompaniment, the repeated 'We love you' appeared to bear little relation to the Stones' usual emphasis on the sexuality of the love experience. [61]

It is not until the end of the song, the slamming of the door, that the message gets through. 'We just came to hound we, and love is all around we.'

"Bang, bang, bang" this big knock at the door which I answered. "Oh, look, there's lots of little ladies and gentlemen outside . . .

We were just gliding off from a twelve-hour trip, and I told one of the women they brought to search the ladies. "Would you mind stepping off that Moroccan cushion. Because you're ruining the tapestries. . ." They tried to get us to turn the record player off and we said, "No. We won't turn it off but we'll turn it down." As they started going out the door, somebody put on *Rainy Day Women* really loud: "Everybody must get stoned". And that was it.

The police did not know about the acid, so it wasn't mentioned at the trial. But the immoral atmosphere, the sweet smell of incense, the naked girl. . .

The judge gave Keith one year's imprisonment and ordered him to pay £500 toward prosecution costs. Frazer was sentenced to six months in jail and £200 costs. 'I sentence you to three months and £100 costs,' the judge said to Mick, who burst into tears.[62]

While the song has a general rhythmic drive and strong delivery, there is, nevertheless, a certain plausibility in the view that the Stones were 'lost in space and hiding under the terrestrial shadow of *Sgt. Pepper*'.[63] The vocal harmonies are similar to those of Lennon/McCartney and initially suggest a sentimentality far removed from the Stones' rough and ready approach, yet the song has an underlying sarcasm. The Beatles had publicly supported the legalisation of drugs. Paul McCartney had made his grand announcement that he took LSD, Brian Epstein had been quoted in *Queen* as being wholeheartedly on the side of hallucinatory drugs and yet neither he nor any of the Beatles was ever 'busted'.[64] In this light the Stones' *We Love You* seems to be more than a simple opportunistic response to the 'summer of love'. It reads more as a rather cynical recognition that the Beatles' *lovable* image was sufficiently well established to allow for a flirtation with either the Maharishi or with LSD. At worst, such behaviour was just being naughty and could be overcome by a simple statement: 'Love, love, love. All you need is love.' *We Love You* seems to reflect Jagger's characteristic pessimistic fatalism: 'Love can't get our minds off [but] We love you, And we hope that you will love "we" too'. Followed by the sound effects of prison doors slamming and seen in relation to the drug trial and the summer of love, the song had the potential to reach more than a No. 10 position on the charts. However, as Christgau points out, the Stones

> never made very convincing hippies because hippie just wasn't their thing . . . Jagger's gift is to make clear that even if the truth doesn't make you free, it needn't sap your will or your energy either . . . He provides the information. The audience must then decide what to do with it.[65]

Within a month the song had disappeared from the charts.

As the *British Record Charts* indicate, with the passing of the summer bands generally moved away from the whimsy of love-based songs towards a more assertive mood, illustrated by the Stones' *Beggar's Banquet*. Donovan alone remained constant to psychedelic love songs, with the albums *Sunshine Superman* (1967) and *A Gift from a Flower to a Garden*. Cream, Pink Floyd and Hendrix also moved away from the limitations of singles.

Scott McKenzie's *San Francisco* and the Flowerpot Men's *Let's Go to San Francisco* seem in retrospect either a requiem for the first phase of hippiedom or a commercialised attempt to promote the American West Coast bands through a popularisation of San Francisco, and in particular the Monterey Festival of June 1967. *San Francisco* had sold well over five million copies in the States alone and in September was at the top of the British record charts.[66] D.A. Pennebaker, who filmed the documentary of Bob Dylan's 1965 tour in England (*Don't Look Back*, 1967) had also taken hours of footage of the Festival, which was made into a full-length documentary, the first to achieve commercial success on an international scale.

By October, The Flowerpot Men's *Let's Go to San Francisco* had risen to No. 8.[67] Written by Carter and Lewis, the song sentimentalises acid by linking it strongly to flower power imagery – 'sunny people walking hand in hand'. The overall effect is persuasively *beautiful*. The mood is relaxed and together with the distancing of the vocal resonates with the reference to *sunshine*, a brand of San Franciscan acid generated to 'make your mind grow . . . up to the sky'. The melody line moves upwards to support the imagery of the flowers that 'grow so very high' with the harmonies achieving a feeling of tension and release through the use of the Cm11–F7–Bb sequence. The song's presentation of San Francisco as a city of beautiful people bore little relation to the hard reality of contemporary events, and the double murder of East Village hippies Linda Fitzpatrick and James 'Groovy' Hutchinson seemed to symbolise the bitter finale of flower power.[68] Rather, it marked only the end of the first phase of glamorising and capitalising on the love ethic and despite its instant success in reaching No. 8 on the charts, the song, like the group, had disappeared within a month.

The popularity of psychedelic rock during 1967 does highlight the fact that the music both symbolically and commercially appealed to a far wider audience than the London-based underground. Clearly the appearance of such bands as Pink Floyd on 'Top of the Pops' made their sound and image more widely known, and as singles both *Arnold Layne* and *See Emily Play* worked at two levels: superficially they were simply quirky and fun, but for those who were attenders at UFO and the Roundhouse they had a deeper meaning which related to a particular psychedelic environment. So both songs simultaneously separated off and bound the counter-culture to a wider network of cultural production and reproduction. Pink Floyd may subsequently have become too experimental for the vague affiliation of the general pop-buying market,[69] but psychedelic music generally had far-reaching repercussions which could not be put down simply to the non-mediated effect of the London underground. Press and television coverage and the effect of such releases as *I Feel Free, Purple Haze* and *The Wind Cries Mary* was both to attract attention to such groups as Cream and the Jimi Hendrix Experience and to project the idea that experimentation with drugs was a part of the whole rock experience. The popularity of psychedelic rock at this time is significant in that it helped to extend the counter-culture's sphere of influence. This was evident in the build-up of the university circuit and underground club network as well as the highly publicised rock festivals, where the most reported aspect was the projection of hippie ideals and the association of particular forms of music with drugs and long-haired youth.

While 1967 points to the widening influence of the counter-culture and the popularising of underground bands, it also highlights the involvement of long-estalished groups with psychedelia. Both the Beatles and the Stones, for example, were sufficiently well established to guarantee a certain receptivity to any new release, but their explicit association with psychedelic rock can be interpreted as legitimising such aspects of the counter-culture as the link between drugs and music and the emphasis on the freedom to experiment, experience and enjoy. The counter-culture was equally aware of the significance of allying itself to the Beatles and the Stones. The Stones were welcomed by the more radical branch of the underground in San Francisco, who hailed them as 'comrades in the desperate battle against the maniacs who hold power. The revolutionary youth of the world hears your music and is inspired to even more deadly acts.' [70]

While the charts of 1967 reflect flower power and its accompanying drug culture, the extent to which the songs would have been *understood* generally as encoding psychedelic experience is impossible to assess. Prior to 1967 the British underground was essentially London based and as such access to songs evoking psychedelic experience was limited. It seems unlikely that the connotations of such early chart singles as *Sunshine Superman* and *I Feel Free* would have been widely recognised. By the summer, however, the coverage by the press of the Stones' trial, the printing of a full-page advertisement in *The Times* calling for the legalisation of marijuana, the glamorisation of the love ethic and the publicity surrounding the Monterey Festival ensured that such songs as *A Whiter Shade of Pale* and *Purple Haze* and Traffic's *Hole in My Shoe* would have been understood to have a connection with drugs. As Middleton and Muncie point out: 'Psychedelic elements in the musical style are typically interpreted as such by reference to a sub-culture of drug-usage; in other words they are defined in this way because hippies said they should be.'[71] To this one could add that psychedelic elements in the musical style are also interpreted as such because of the publicity surrounding them.

The fact that pyschedelic rock attracted both a wide audience and such groups as the Move and the Stones emphasises the point that whatever its initial cultural focus, a musical form can run outwards in many directions. The counter-culture's distinction between 'serious music, music for *living* by *and* music for *leisure*'[72] crystallises the way in which social reality and music were perceived as fusing to create a collective experience with revolutionary potential. The trivialisation of psychedelia through such formulaic singles as *Let's Go to San Francisco* may be one reason why groups such as Cream and Pink Floyd moved so strongly against top twenty and commercial music. Valued by the underground for their progressive ideas and techniques, their chart ratings indicate that during the summer of 1967 neither the groups nor their music were the exclusive property of the counter-culture. It is significant that after 1967 both Cream and Pink Floyd produced albums in which artistic integrity was the basis of commercial success. In doing so, they created a new market which, while carrying the stigma of being highly commercial, was nevertheless valued by the counter-culture as sufficiently differentiated to prevent diffusion by the hip entrepreneurs whose ability to deflect the radical implications of musical styles was so much in evidence in the marketing of psychedelic rock/pop.

There was strong reaction from the underground to the popularising of psychedelic rock. The Electric Garden, one of the more extravagant of the psychedelic venues, was quickly annexed, renamed Middle Earth and kept firmly shut on UFO nights. Such sensationalised love-ins as the Alexandra Palace's 'Twenty Four Hour Technicolour Dream' and the Duke of Bedford's Woburn Abbey Festival of the Flower Children were cynically dubbed 'cash-ins' by the underground, who ran their own events in Slough, Hull and Glastonbury in the summer of '67. Jim Haynes launched his experimental workshop in Drury Lane in July 1967 and by 1969 over 150 arts lab organisations had been announced, to be linked by a videotape network and financed by a trust.

It seems that the popularising of acid rock hardened the underground's determination to preserve its own identity; in relation to this, Willis's identification of *Sgt. Pepper* as a turning point in choice of environment is interesting.[73] The fact that the Beatles had become 'Underground converts' was newsworthy: their changed image and the attendant emphasis on love and drugs inevitably stimulated comment and imitation but the extent to which this accompanied any real change in life style is impossible to assess. Rather the album seemed to separate the more innovatory singles of January–July from such commercialised hits as *San Francisco* and *Let's Go to San Francisco*, so providing a symbolic point in the move towards 'larger forms, oppositions and variations'[74] which were less susceptible to exploitation. The focus on concept albums seemed to draw on the collective experience of *Sgt. Pepper*, which provided a musical equivalent of the community already established by the Monterey Festival and such London underground bases as UFO and the Roundhouse.[75]

While the trivialisation of Flower Power and the success of such singles as *Let's Go to San Francisco* initially appeared to undermine the more revolutionary aims of psychedelia – change the prevailing mode of consciousness and you change the world – as Richard Neville points out,

> The hippie movement wasn't dead, of course, it was merely the end of the phase of press glamorization. . . . In that busy October month of 1967, while flower power wilted, a new movement was born. . . . This was the Youth International Party. It was not to hit the headlines until August 1968.[76]

Easter 1968 saw the shooting of Rudi Dutschke as he left the Berlin headquarters of the German Socialist Students' Federation. By May, in almost every other West European city there were exchange centres for underground newspapers, massive pop-music freak-outs, communal crash pads and a billowing hash scene.[77] In England, three students were arrested after demonstrations at Essex University. Hornsey and Guildford students occupied their respective art colleges and Britain's underground, while generally ambivalent about such disruptions, sensed an affinity of purpose which resulted in an explosion of arts laboratories. In terms of music, however, the only direct reference to the student revolution and the battle of Grosvenor Square came from the Beatles, in *Revolution* (1968):

> You say you'll change the constitution
> Well, you know we all want to change your head

and the Stones in *Street Fighting Man*. However, as Middleton and Muncie point out, the politics of the British counter-culture was largely a 'cultural politics'; to most of those involved, the fight was not on the level of political system, but on that of personal freedom: the freedom to experience and enjoy.[78] As such, psychedelic experience falls into place as one, but only one, possible method of mounting that exploration. It becomes a limited chemical means to a greater psychic end, namely the reformulation of the personality, upon which social ideology and culture generally are ultimately based.[79]

5   The Rolling Stones

The distinction between 'serious music, music for living by and music for leisure'[1] was of fundamental importance to the counter-culture and highlights the way in which social reality and musical experience fused into a collective experience. While 1967 focused 'love' as a weapon with revolutionary potential, the overt sexuality and underlying violence in performance and musical style associated with such performers as Jimi Hendrix, the Stones, the Doors, Love and MC5 initially seem at variance with a movement committed to peace and love. Further, whilst it might be argued that on stage the groups' sexual aggression was little more than formalised and ritualised violence, the music nevertheless has a neurotic element which, in its more frenzied form, evokes a pseudo-tribal paranoia. 'Rob Tyner, the MC5 lead singer, sprints on stage, leaps high in the air, his body writhing through the strobes: then as he hits ground: KICK OUT THE JAMS, MOTHERFUCKERS!'[2] There was, then, an obverse side to the notion of love more consonant with the 'hedonism and self-gratification', 'social irreverence and an interest in experimental ways of life', of certain groups within the counter-culture.

Any society contains an endemic violence which can surface via the musical constructs of the period, whether it be Stravinsky (*The Rite of Spring*) or the Crazy World of Arthur Brown (*Fire*). Even so, it would appear that certain counter-cultural groups took a position somewhat similar to that of William Burroughs' *Naked Lunch* in their moral demonicism, and that the combination of drugs and music provided a route to the tension and eroticism at the other end of the emotional spectrum. Analogous, perhaps, to the total instinctual liberation preached by the more extreme hippy communities, there was an emphasis on the annihilation of individual consciousness linked to personal freedom and subjective experience.[3]

This loss of consciousness might at first seem somewhat of a contradiction to the programme of change inherent in underground manifestoes.[4] Constructive political action and confrontation appear to be negated by an emphasis on spontaneous response and lack of rationality.[5] Yet there is a certain homology with the politics of the Youth International Party, whose strategy of revolution moved towards an attack on the establishment through aesthetic politics – mocking militarism, exorcising the Pentagon, throwing money on to the floor of the New York Stock Exchange and nominating a pig for President.

Initially there appears to be an underlying tension between the political activism of the student New Left and the 'Fuck the System' bohemianism of the hippies and the yippies. At a deeper level, however, both extremes were united in their attack on the traditional institutions which reproduce dominant cultural-ideological relations – the family, education, media, marriage and the sexual division of labour. There was a shared emphasis on the freedom to question and experiment, a commitment to personal action and an intensive examination of the self. This common viewpoint, a *consciousness* within the counter-culture, involved more than a simple dogma or ideology in its emphasis on introspection, pleasure and optimism.[6]

As Roszak points out:

> Beat-hip bohemianism may be too withdrawn from social action to suit New Left radicalism; but the withdrawal is in a direction the activist can readily understand. The 'trip' (for example) is inward, towards deeper levels of self-examination. The easy transition from one wing to the other of the counter culture shows up in the pattern that has come to govern many of the free universities. These dissenting academies usually receive their send-off from campus New Left Activists and initially emphasize heavy politics. But gradually the curricula tend to get hip both in content and teaching methods: psychedelics, light shows, multi-media, total theatre, people-heaping, McLuhan, exotic religion, touch and tenderness, ecstatic laboratories. . . . We see the underlying unity of the counter-cultural variety, then, if we see beat-hip bohemianism as an effort to work out the personality and total life style that follow from New Left social criticism. At their best, these young bohemians are the would-be utopian pioneers of the world that lies beyond intellectual rejection of the Great Society. They seek to invent a cultural base for New Left politics, to discover new types of community, new family patterns, new sexual mores, new kinds of livelihood, new esthetic forms, new personal identities on the far side of power politics, the bourgeois home, and the consumer society.[7]

So the search for personal identity and the acceptance of chaos and uncertainty can be interpreted as a prelude to rebirth, the ego temporarily destroyed before moving on to a changed form of consciousness. The Grateful Dead, for example, were referring to such an experience in their adopted name,[8] which also reflected their attitude of profound dissatisfaction with being *alive* in Reagan's California at the time: the state of the *outside* reality of Vietnam and the police violence against protesters at Berkeley. Similarly, Jimi Hendrix's playing of the *Star-Spangled Banner* on his *Woodstock* album as the introduction to *Purple Haze* focuses on changed consciousness. 'He does not do it as José Feliciano sang it at the World Series. He does it screwing the guitar and it is, I submit, a revolutionary act.'[9] This juxtaposition focuses on the use of LSD as providing new insights and referential points. 'After an acid trip you can reject everything you have ever been taught . . . the world becomes a circus with the emphasis on parody.'[10] Yet as Joel Fort points out, mood change can be unpleasant as well as pleasant,[11] leading to a rediscovery of forgotten instinctual depths and the release of the demonic; personal freedom then equates with the more extreme forms of self-gratification.[12] When LSD was married to unremitting beat and noise, the end result could be both upsetting and disruptive with the combination of egocentricity and drug/music-induced tribal unity leading to mass eroticism and/or violence.

> The Doors. Their style is cunnilingual with overtones of the Massacre of the Innocents. An electrified sex slaughter. A musical blood-bath. . . . The Doors are carnivores in a land of musical vegetarians . . . their talons, fangs and folded wings are seldom out of view, but if they leave us crotch-raw and exhausted, at least they leave us aware of our aliveness. And of our destiny. The Doors scream into the darkened auditorium what all of us in the underground are whispering more softly in our hearts: we want the world and we want it . . . NOW![13]

While the banner 'Make Love Not War', with its emphasis on gentle eroticism and the cultivation of feminine softness as a political stand against the traditional he-manliness of political life,[14] may be viewed as one of the most remarkable aspects of the counter-culture, the fight against middle-class prurience led increasingly towards an explicit identification of sexual freedom with total freedom. Underground newspapers such as *Screw*, *Oz*, *IT*, *East Village Other*, *The Seed*, *Evergreen Review* and *Fucknam* made use of obscenity as a popular pretext for confrontation between Authority and the Movement. As Richard Neville points out:

> Obscenity is traditionally among the armoury of weapons employed by the alienated and frustrated. What is different about 'man fined for making obscene remarks about Premier', the *Book of Rugby Songs*, Jonathan Swift and the manic bawdiness of today's militants, is that the latter use it *en masse* intersexually, instinctively, not only to entertain their listeners but as a matter of policy to communicate animosity to their enemies *and* love for each other.[15]

The use of pornography was often justified in terms of its boisterous, self-directed humour ('*Screw* is a two-bit whore') or as *playpower* ('Female Fuckability Test'),[16] but the fact that *The Berkeley Barb* regularly carried at least three pages of advertising for blue movies along with a vast amount of 'velvet underground' (soft porn) classified ads moved against any such notion of satire. As Roszak points out: 'Such obscenity merchandisers make about as much of a contribution to sexual freedom as the Strategic Air Command – whose motto is "peace is our profession" – makes to healthy international relations.'[17] So while love was fundamental to all branches of the counter-culture there was nevertheless a marked difference between the transcendental spirituality promised to the followers of the Majarishi Mahesh Yogi and the revolutionary liberation of the Yippie Party's Jerry Rubin and his symbolic call for patricide.

These apparently opposing philosophies are also reflected in the ethos of rock. If its function is seen as liberating repressions and allowing its audience to reflect on their dissatisfaction with society and the problems that drive people apart, then the movement towards a communality based on love would appear a logical development. If, however, chaos and uncertainty are recognised as a legitimate and necessary part of life, and if these concerns hinge on the notion of repressed sexuality, then the conjunction with sensuality and death appears logical. Marcuse and Brown, major social theorists among the disaffiliated young of Western Europe and America, both recognised the human body as 'the perennial battlefield where the war of instincts is waged' and that alienation was primarily psychic, not sociological.[18] While Marcuse saw liberation as the achievement of a 'libidinal rationality', freedom within sensible limits rather than total liberation, Brown takes the argument further. In his reading of Freud it is the peculiarly human awareness and rejection of death, man's anxiety in the face of his own mortality, that is fundamental:

> The energy of our history making is derived from the tension between the life and death instincts as they carry on their neurotic project of rejecting one another. When this energy is used in a socially acceptable way, we have 'sublimation' – that desexualisation of conduct on which Freud pinned so much of his hope for the survival of civilization. But underlying all forms of sublimation, as well as the recognized neuroses, there is the same antagonism of the instincts, the mutual thrusting away which finally segregates the death instinct and drives it into its independent career as the dark terror . . .[19]

History is thus defined in terms of the struggle to fill time with death-defying works. In Brown's view, as long as we continue to pit life against death we perpetuate the ontological dilemma of humanity: 'the death instinct is reconciled with the life instinct only in a life which is not repressed, which leaves no "unlived lives" in the human body, the death instinct then being affirmed in a body which is willing to die'.[20]

It could be argued that the emphasis on death and/or satanic ritual, which characterised the performance of such apparently disparate groups as the Doors, Alice Cooper, Frank Zappa and the Rolling Stones, had a certain affinity with contemporary thinking. The US West Coast band, Love, for example, led by Arthur Lee, lived on a disused Hollywood set (non-reality) and were rumoured to have slit the throats of their roadies but were never brought to trial. They became a cult band among the extremists in the counter-culture, with such songs as *Hey Joe* and *Little Red Book* exhibiting a brooding and menacing style in the muttered vocals and sensual guitar style. Sex and death motifs were of fundamental importance to the image of the Doors, while Alice Cooper would chop up dolls and use props like electric chairs, boa constrictors and gallows in performance. Love, the Doors and Cooper provide one example of the possible relationship between particular forms of music and adopted philosophies. Yet it is debatable whether the groups exhibited either an instinctual or thought-through expression of prevalent theories.[21] It is more likely that by 1968–9 certain images had become common property. The Beatles, for example, could project the dilemmas of contemporary society, the paranoias, the social distress, and set up an alternative framework of love as the way to reconstitute a sense of community. The whole concept of love and communality comes through in *Yellow Submarine*, which was frequently sung at demonstrations as an expression of solidarity. The deliberate mystification of *A Whiter Shade of Pale* was seen as expressing psychedelic/mystical experience because the counter-culture had sufficiently established the importance of visionary mysticism through such writers as Ginsberg with his emphasis on Zen.

While rock music may have been the aesthetic form most closely bound up with sexual experience, and for the counter-culture rock groups were the real 'prophets' of the movement,[22] the problem still arises of how rock, as an ideological and cultural form, plays a role in the way in which its users constituted their sexuality. *My Little Red Book*, for example, was a Bacharach–David song first performed by Manfred Mann in *What's New Pussycat?* In Love's hands, the lyrics were the same, but the style became altogether more potent and sensual, illustrating how rock as a cultural form has many layers of meaning which can be expressed in performance. The message of the lyrics may be undercut by rhythmic or melodic conventions; mikes and guitars can be used as phallic symbols; the music itself can build towards techniques of arousal and climax which, when allied to the sexual frankness of the rhythm, can move towards a total assertion of male sexual iconography. At this point, the virtuosity associated with progressive rock approaches a statement of sexual skill and domination. 'Jimi Hendrix leaves little doubt as to which sensory organ his guitar is an extension of (forcing TV cameras to feign obsessive interest in his face).'[23]

So while musical structures generate meaning, particular attitudes were also valued in counter-cultural strategy.

The musician . . . gives himself up to his product in almost exhibitionistic fashion. He lives it out in public, as it were, in the act of performance, with every movement and gesture of his body. He celebrates the ritual whereby the fetish of sound is to be venerated. Hence, too, the pronounced cult of spontaneity in the aesthetics of rock music, since spontaneous self-expression seemed to contain the secret element capable of endowing mere sound with the 'at the same time perceptible and imperceptible' force of a mode of social liberation.[24]

The Fugs, for example, started out as a random collection of poets, some of whom decided to sing. From the start their intention was to free the senses by shocking audiences with poetry, satire and often gross obscenity. Their début album, released in 1965, contained ten of their less offensive songs and was effectively the first of what would later be called 'underground' music. Identified with marijuana, pacifism, satire and sexual invention, they were the fathers of the Mothers of Invention, who with Frank Zappa enlarged the possibilities of rock to include extended audience participation.[25]

The association of political progressivism and cultural subversion with overt sexuality may well be the reason why the Rolling Stones were acclaimed by the more militant branches of the counter-culture. With the recognition of rock as a means of liberation for the young from adult repressions, the Stones' sexuality was seen as a challenge to the establishment. Their confrontational style equated with sexual freedom, relating strongly to the senses. The adjectives (such as 'brutal, menacing, erectile, tough, obscene, nightmarish, outrageous') which accompanied reviews of their performances, can also be pinned to Hendrix, the Doors, the Grateful Dead, Frank Zappa, MC5 and the Fugs. The celebration of love and freedom had, then, its darker side and as Roszak points out,

> even when crudity is meant to satirize or reply in kind to the corruptions of the dominant culture, there is bound to come a point where sardonic imitation destroys the sensibilities and produces simple callousness. . . . How is one to make certain that the exploration of the non-intellective powers will not degenerate into a maniacal nihilism?[26]

Do more frenetic forms of rock predispose their audience towards particular forms of action? If the reception of music becomes converted into a symbolic act of self-liberation and self-realisation through which the individual can find a way back to the self as a value and potentiality, then the fact that certain groups come across as destructive and overtly sexual is an important factor in the analysis of meaning attributed to music by the counter-culture. As Simon Frith points out:

> rock can't just be consumed, but must be responded to like any other form of art – its tensions and contradictions engaged and reinterpreted into the listeners' experience. Such engagement is intellectual and moral, the results are enriching and can be disturbing . . . The rock audience is not seen as a passive mass, consuming records like cornflakes but as an active community making music into a symbol of solidarity and an inspiration for action.[27]

The problem arises of whether the frenetic energy of groups like the Stones can motivate instability; whether the sexuality and obsessive violence of such songs as *Jumpin' Jack Flash*, *Brown Sugar*, *Midnight Rambler* and *Sympathy for the Devil* can lead to violence.

> 'I [Jagger] don't understand the connection between music and violence,' he has said – a trifle disingenuously. 'I just know that I get very aroused by music, but that it doesn't arouse me violently. I never went to a rock 'n' roll show and wanted to smash windows or beat anybody up afterwards. I feel more sexual than actually physically violent.'[28]

The superimposition of a particular piece of music on to a suitably predisposed mind is clearly essential in musical communication. Equally it can be an essential component in social interaction, since a musical language embodies the social and intellectual structure of a society. So can the events at Altamont be attributed to a mixture of acid and obsessively violent music; were the Stones simply expressing something important about society – how society *is* – or were they offering an alternative way of life, a mode of protest? *Satisfaction*, for example, can be read as a rejection by Jagger of the orthodox neoclassical economics training he received during his brief undergraduate days at the London School of Economics. This school of thought, which is still dominant after one hundred years, claims that the rational consumer pursues as his goal 'the maximisation of satisfaction', albeit under constraints. The song can be read either as anticipating a post-scarcity society, thereby undermining the notion of constraints (the song must be seen against the phase of rapid economic growth that Eric Hobsbawm has called 'The Long Boom') or as challenging the notion of 'satisfaction' as an end in itself.[29] The song also establishes the insatiable sexual appetite of Jagger himself.

Dominated equally by Jagger's assertive delivery and Keith Richards' lead guitar riff with which the song opens, the bare texture is underlined both by the acerbic and tinny sound of the lead guitar and the deliberate punctuation on rhythm guitar which works to establish the powerful four-in-a-bar beat.

The verse is just as bare in texture, with the harsh timbres on the guitars reflected in Jagger's delivery. While the vocal line is fragmented, the slow triplet rhythm of the opening words ('I can't get no satisfaction') move against and frustrate the relentless flow of the four-beat time to provide tension. This is accentuated by the way in which Jagger initially breathes the words into the microphone before moving into an arrogant and pro-gressively more dominant 'Cause I try, and I try, and I try and I try'.

There is a strong sense of arousal in the ascending sequence on 'and I try' which is brought to a climax on the 'I can't get no. . .'. While the lead guitar stresses the rhythm of the words through strongly accented chords, the rhythm guitar returns to the opening riff, increasing the level of excitement through a precise and calculated rhythm which works to undercut the lyrics' 'losing streak'.

The insistent pulsating guitar riff and the threatening 'I can't get no satisfaction' makes it apparent that no female present is capable of satisfying Jagger's sexual drive. In performance, conquests are counted and in his most overtly sexual and preening manner Jagger rounds on the audience: 'and I tried [you – pointing to one] and I tried [you – to another] and I tried [you].' This mood of aggressive sexuality was heightened in Jagger's late sixties tours when a huge inflated phallus provided a visual analogy for his narcissistic yet threatening performance.

While the Stones expressed no specific identification with the counter-culture, they may have been influenced both by the London underground with its focus on the psychedelic and by the wide coverage of the Monterey Festival. At the same time, their importance and reputation in the rock world was instrumental in setting up themes of cultural meanings; for example their insistence on 'doing your own thing' resonated with the late 1960s ideology of artistic freedom and self-expression. The focus on frustration and satisfaction in relation to personal and sexual relations mirrored the views of the underground element which most strongly identified sexual freedom and total freedom. Recognised by the extreme left of the underground as an inspiration to 'even more deadly acts': as liberators and 'bearers of the message',[30] the Stones' cultural subversion made them appear natural allies.

The Stones' commitment to sex, dope and lavish autonomy[31] can be seen as a betrayal of

all the flaws of the counter culture they half-wittingly and willingly symbolised. Their sex was too often sexist, their expanded consciousness too often a sordid escape; their rebellion rooted in impulse to the exclusion of all habit of sacrifice and their relationships to fame had little to do with the responsibilities of leadership or of allegiance.[32]

This lack of responsibility is reflected in their attitude towards their fans. Jagger's statement following the Harker trial may refer to drug usage, but it also shows his belief in the autonomy of the individual:

As far as I am concerned we did pretty well because we never said everyone should take this or that. We never said you shouldn't. We just left it up to everyone else which is the way it should be. Which is my version of responsibility.[33]

The Stones' songs, their personal stance against society and their huge sense of uncompromised independence indicate an individualistic rather than a corporate stance. There is a certain echo of the counter-culture's commitment to personal action, the freedom to question, the emphasis on permissiveness and the public flouting of the *normal* codes of convention, but any straightforward identification was tempered by an opportunistic willingness to capitalise on their image as evil genius, even if it entailed a certain compromise in style.

This compromise comes through most clearly in *Their Satanic Majesties Request*, ostensibly the record which linked them most strongly with the psychedelic, but which was regarded by critics as 'toothless . . . and boring. It wasn't freakish or dire or nauseous – it was a drag. It had no rage or arrogance left. No image.' [34]

The 'no image' is clearly contentious. Like the Beatles' *Sgt. Pepper*, the image is there on the cover sleeve. The Stones *pose* as magicians among swirling psychedelic patterns. The juxtaposed images on the centre spread, the paraphernalia of black magic, ostensibly interpolate the *aficionado* of both the Stones and the satanic edge of the counter-culture itself. The result is heavily posed and suggests a conscious and complementary response to the *Sgt. Pepper* image of the Beatles. Throughout their career the Stones had been an often deliberate contrast to the Beatles, following each move with a reciprocal response: 'Selfish, spiteful and sexually threatening, they stirred subliminal feelings that popular music preferred to leave alone, but which in black music had always been closer to the surface.' [35]

The opening track on *Satanic Majesties* is similar in technique to that of *Sgt. Pepper* in that it attempts to draw the audience into the mood of the record. There is a quasi-cacophony of sound which evokes memories of *A Day in the Life*. The sound functions narratively. Electronically distorted piano chords are interrupted by jangling brass to suggest the jangling tensions of the 'outside' world before the simplicity of the chant-like chorus. An up-beat tempo and directness of expression elicits a pre-conditioned response to the invitation:

Why don't we sing this song
All together?

The lyrics draw heavily on psychedelic imagery. There is the offer of an alternative experience, a celebration of *life* which is in direct opposition to the stress of the outside world implied by the opening sounds of the song. Rather than 'open our *minds*', we are invited to 'open our *heads*', implying an anti-intellectual collective response which pulls both on the primeval imagery of the verse and the promise of expanded metaphysical experience through LSD:

And if we close all our eyes together
Then we will see where we all come from.

With symbolic communication established, the song moves into the verse, the change of key providing a musical metaphor for movement into the 'trip' which is reinforced by the distanced vocal and hazy timbres. Suggested points of reference, the 'pictures', work on the subconscious to evoke both a synaesthetic response and a sense of communality before the brass inter-jects, calling the initiate deeper into hallucinogenic experience. Here the sounds carry the information. The tabla suggests the metaphysical journey, the incessant, drum rhythm giving a sense of continuity as fragmentary motifs on piano, guitar and bells move in and out of focus.

The second and third verses take the listener deeper into the past:

Pictures of us beating on our drums
Never stopping till the rain has come.

Pictures of us spin the circling sun
Pictures of us show that we're all one . . .

There is a solidarity similar to that established by the opening chorus of the Beatles' *Sgt. Pepper*, but instead of a past established 'twenty years ago today', we are taken further back, to the beginning of time. The incessant drumbeat suggests a primeval community where man has the power to make rain and, with the given image of Jagger as magician, there is a foregrounding of the black arts. The Stones, it is implied, have the power to take us back to an alternative past, one diametrically opposed to that shown by the Beatles who, in contrast, are portrayed on the album sleeve as 'flower children', their heads framed by coloured daisies.

All Together finishes abruptly on a noisy Bb/B on brass to provide a blue-note dominant entry into *The Citadel*. The technique is similar to that established in *Sgt. Pepper*, where the chorus ends with the announcement of 'The one and only Billy Shears', which follows without break against thunderous applause from 'the audience'. This time, there is no such need for an introduction, for the strident r&b style and menacing vocal delivery is immediately recognisable as *The Rolling Stones*.

The vocal, based on a repetitive motif with an almost incantatory effect, simultaneously denounces and celebrates capitalism:

Flags are flying dollar bills
From the heights of concrete hills

The effect is of power and a certain decadence with the words rebounding against the inherent sexuality of the r&b rhythm. The mood is reinforced by the invitation in the lyrics to Candy and Cathy. Here the voice is fronted, the tone of address suggesting a sexual interpretation of *well*ness ('hope you both are well'). This is reinforced by the 'Please come and see me' and the momentary pause before 'in the citadel' where the words are breathed into the microphone.

Initially there appears to be conflict between an apparent denouncement of inequality:

In the streets of many walls
Here the peasants come and crawl
You can hear their numbers called

and Jagger's sensual delivery. There is little sense of pity or outrage; instead the song suggests a complicity with the 'Screaming people' and the 'shiny metal cars' with the band's high-decibel approach feeding the connotations of the words. There is continuity here, as Jagger's denouncement of social and political breakdown/inequality had always been delivered through a combination of irony and ecstasy. As Merton points out: 'The enormous merit and audacity of The Stones [was] to have repeatedly and consistently defied the central taboos of society.' They had 'done so in the most radical and unacceptable way possible: by *celebrating* it. The light this black beam throws on society is too bright for it. Nakedly proclaimed, inequality is *de facto* denounced.' [36]

In contrast, *In Another Land* draws heavily on the psychedelic, both in musical language and in lyrics. The introduction, played on harpsichord supported by descending octaves on the organ, is played twice with the chords providing a musical metaphor for the route into the subconscious.

Electronically produced wind effects are introduced to create a sensation of space which continues into the verse, where the distancing of the voice line picks up on the idea of *space*. The melody line is relaxed, the note values simply following the inflections of the words as if to convey the naturalness of the trip. The use of rests and held notes on 'Land' and 'hand' allow the listener to reflect on the new experiences. Supported by a gently moving harpsichord accompaniment over ghost-like chords on the organ, the mood is one of non-reality, an impression enhanced by the use of white noise and other electronic sound effects. Subtle changes of colour are created through unpredictable modulations which work against the initial V–I cadence to support the feeling of insubstantiality; the shifting harmonies prevent the listener from anticipating the direction the song is to take, providing instead a dreamy vagueness and underlying gentleness, with the musical structures supporting the words:

> where the breeze and trees and the flowers were blue. . .
> and the spray flew high and the feathers floated by

There is a simultaneous feeling of support in the chorused, 'ahhhhh' over 'I stood and held your hand' and the duetted 'And nobody else's hand will ever do', which is reassuring to the inexperienced LSD user disturbed by a change in consciousness: 'I didn't know how I came to be here and not asleep in bed.'

The electronic distortion of the voice, the distancing effects, the blurred timbres and the white sound combine to form a musical analogy to the hallucinatory state suggested by the words. Perceptual changes are foregrounded by the gentle pace and shifting chord structure.

This hallucinatory state is abruptly broken by a *wide awake* chorus in heavy r&b style (see example 8). The contrast with the opening section is marked and suggests a far more 'awake' sound in the shouted-out vocals. The texture is less differentiated and it is often difficult to distinguish guitar, piano and cymbals which together push towards an uncompromised density of sound which is dominated by rhythm. The most atypical sound is Charlie Watts' drumming, which displays an unusual amount of frills.

As a whole, the effect is jangly with treble sound predominating on the amplified acoustic guitar. This is enhanced by the trebly piano which is mixed in quietly with cymbals. The contrast between the quiet serenity of the verse and the strident chorus is effective in creating a musical equivalent of non-reality and reality. The psychedelic experience is shown to be gentle, there is time to reflect and focus on the colours. Nothing is violent, the feathers float, the grass grows high. In contrast the chorus is more abrasive and although the questions are spaced out the pulsating rhythm moves towards a sense of arousal which is initially satisfied by a return to the verse. The final 'I opened up my eyes and much to my surprise', however, ends in heavy breathing and snoring.

So there is a certain ironic distancing. The Stones could take on the psychedelic, use similar techniques to Floyd (the use of white sound, for example, appears in *Astronomy Dominé* to evoke a similar feeling of space) and the Beatles (the chorusing over 'hand' and 'land', the use of harpsichord and unpredictable chord progressions in *Strawberry Fields Forever*), and juxtapose the trip with the reality of their own r&b-based sound to produce

Example 8 In Another Land

Example 8 cont.

what is arguably an innovative track but could still sit back from the result. So did the Stones find the excursion into a psychedelic musical framework a necessary but boring obligation?[37]

2000 Man, while hinting at the psychedelic – 'And I grow tiny flow'rs in my little window sill' – is a strong r&b track which focuses on alienation. The verse cynically attacks the 'age of technology':

Well, my name is a number, a piece of plastic film

While there is continuity in Jagger's anti-woman stance, the real rage is directed against the way in which the person is denied in favour of the machine:

Well, my wife still respects me, I really misuse her
I am having an affair with a random computer

The chorus extends the definition of alienation to the generation gap. Underpinned by a strongly rhythmic bass riff the vocal hovers between F# and G, the fierce delivery, harsh timbres and thudding beat undercutting the pride in planet and sun (son) suggested by the words. Here there is a parallel with *Satisfaction* in the clash between literal sense and interpretation through performance. Jagger expresses both rage and virility. There is no real expression of filial interest ('Oh, Daddy, is your brain still flashing like it did when you were young?') but a characteristic mocking irony which is heightened by the momentary delay between 'your' and 'brain'. The implications of 'flashing' allied to delivery suggest both the impotency of the father and the potency of the son.

Although this is reminiscent of the Beatles' exploration of alienation in *Nowhere Man*, the underlying aggression in *2000 Man* appears more realistic in its view of the rift between generations. There is no feeling that *love* can show the way, rather a hostile recognition that the evils of society are attributable to the preceding generation's emphasis on technocracy. The attack reflects this generational antagonism towards the expansion of technocracy and the nearly pathological passivity of the parent generation, unwilling to combat large-scale capitalistic enterprise. One significant example of repressive desublimation (i.e. the way in which technocracy generates submission and weakens the rationality of protest) is sexuality. To liberate sexuality would be to create a society in which technocratic discipline would be impossible. To thwart sexuality outright would create a widespread, explosive resentment that would require policing.[38] Jagger's mocking cynicism in his identification of the impotence of the parent generation, the celebration of the ethos of disaffiliation through rock, equates with the politics of the counter-culture. Within the context of the album and following the psychedelic *In Another Land*, *2000 Man* reads as a rejection of the norms of the dominant culture, with the power in the music and the delivery working to liberate the young from adults' repressions.

The first side of the album concludes with nearly eight minutes of jumbled sounds, interrupted conversations – 'all those flowers', 'where's that joint', pantings and vaguely Indian-sounding chanting, drumming, sighs and moans which gradually lead to a reprise of *Sing This All Together*. This is the Stones at their least convincing. If the sounds are meant to symbolise changed states of consciousness after taking LSD, then there is no sense of assurance. Ending on an electronically distorted 'We wish you a merry Christmas' the track reinforces the impression that the Stones are least successful when they are *trying* to be counter-cultural. What they do best, and when they are genuinely subversive, is when they carry bourgeois norms to such extremes that they horrify society.[39]

The idea that the Stones were attempting to oppose the communality established by the Beatles on *Sgt. Pepper* by using similar organisational techniques (the opening track, side one, complex sound mixes, sound montages and psychedelic coding) is also in evidence on side two, track 1. Again the audience is drawn into the album through a montage of voices which create the atmosphere of a street market, the vendor inviting the crowd to play the game 'one spin only, any prize'. The mood of camaraderie is not unlike that evoked in *Being For the Benefit of Mr. Kite!*[40] The world is the world of show biz, but unlike the Beatles' where the focus is on the psychedelic circus, the prize offered by the Stones is a soul. With this suggestion in mind the theme is established, but the following track has only an obscure sense of contextual continuity. Initially the song reads like an attempt to reconstruct *Lucy in the Sky with Diamonds*. Both women draw on colour associations. *Lucy*, 'the girl with kaleidoscope eyes', lives in a world of 'cellophane flowers of yellow and blue'. In the Stones' version 'she comes in colours everywhere . . . she combs her hair, she's like a rainbow, combing colours in the air'.

While *She's a Rainbow* has a certain similarity to *Lady Jane*, the lyrics appear to be so far removed from the Stones' usual ferocious and voracious attitude towards women that the effect is contrived. *Lady Jane* may disguise the use of women in a persuasively lyrical ballad form, but 'dear Lady Anne' and 'sweet Marie' are still enjoyed and left.[41] In contrast, *She's a Rainbow* evokes the beauty and mystery of women, drawing heavily on the poetic language of Donovan in the simplicity of the lyrics and the melody line. An Alberti-like introduction suggests an uncharacteristic classic restraint reminiscencent of Mozart. The opening chorus, however, has more rhythmic attack in the punchy bass line, yet there is still a basic simplicity of texture. The emphasis is on melody and the voice is fronted against a rhythmic/ harmonic accompaniment.

The chorus is sung twice, separated by a recapitulation of the introduction which is then extended to form a link with the verse. Lyrical violins and cellos are introduced in the background which add romanticism to the otherwise restrained piano line. The verse picks up on the first bar of the piano line, the upward movement of the line conjuring up images of sky, rainbow, moon and sunset.

This comes across as a carefully orchestrated ballad. The vocal line, 'have you seen a lady fairer', has a modified version of the opening bar of the chorus. The use of violins and cellos recall the Beatles' *She's Leaving Home* and *Strawberry Fields Forever* and the Alberti-style introduction reflects one of the trends in 1967, towards rock/classical fusion.[42] At the same time, the jittery breakdown at the end of the song, the scraping strings on the cello and violins, the distanced tolling bells, have a similar retrospective effect to the mounting climax in *Mr. Kite*, the leery laugh at the end of *Within You Without You*, the unexpected ending of *Good Morning*.[43] *She's a Rainbow* might be a romanticised vision of a woman, but 'she shoots colours all around' provides an alternative image in its evocation of fixing. Opium-based drugs may transport the user upwards: 'What a resurrection from the lowest depths of the inner spirit!'[44] but the withdrawal symptoms are painful. At this point, the focus of the opening track becomes clear. She can provide ecstasy, peace of mind, but the price might be a soul.

The Lantern initially echoes the arpeggios of *She's a Rainbow*. Introduced by distanced chimes, an acoustic guitar and distanced flute lead into a blues-like introduction. The verse then moves into a strongly fronted vocal with barrel house-style link bars. There is an enigmatic quality in the way in which the beat recedes from the foreground as Jagger sings out:

We, in our present life. . .
You, cross the sea of night. . .

and comes back again in the link passages. There are parallels here with the Grateful Dead, who use similar techniques in *Live Dead* to effect a sense of transition between the two states. The focus on the lantern implies an alternative meaning in its evocation of a guiding spirit: 'The cloak you wear is a spirit shroud, You'll wake me in my sleeping hours.' The barrel-house accompaniment is essentially earth-bound in its links with bar and brothel while the blues give a sense of comfort: 'I love the blues because the blues is the only thing that gives me relief when I gets to the place where it seems like everything go wrong.'[45] There is then a possible progression. *Like a Rainbow* ends in dissonance, the hint of withdrawal from heroin. *The Lantern* carries the idea further through the focus on 'me in my sorry plight'. Death waits: 'you hear the stopping of my heart, we never part, so please carry the lantern high'.

Within the concept of the metaphysical journey – the acceptance of death and uncertainty as a prelude to rebirth, the ego temporarily destroyed before moving on to a changed form of consciousness – the final four-second pause takes on a new significance. Symbolically the audience have arrived at a state of awareness, which is musically encoded in the following track. *Gomper* opens with an electronically distanced organ introduction supported by tabla, sitar and gently intoned chanting. The change from the normal timbres of the previous song implies an alternative experience. Supported by the plangent, sustained quality of the sitar and a gently rocking bass, the vocal gently intones 'By the lake with lily flowers, while away the evening hours.'

Based on a vocal riff, with a repetitive bass line and an echo-like effect between the melody line and the two-bar sitar link, the cumulative effect is strangely mesmeric. The combination of repetition with the bright timbres suggests a trance which is initially broken by the fronting of the voice in the second section, the change in accompaniment and the suggestion of voyeurism in 'The sun sees her dried, the birds hover high, I stifle a cry.'

The trance-like state is then restored in the solo break and the final sitar coda which builds on the introduction with increasing intensity before a low chord on organ, followed by electronically distorted chords, moves the listener deeper into space. Over the continuous rhythmic throb of the bass and focused by splashes of electronic colour, Jagger describes a journey into space, *2000 Light Years from Home*. Word painting is effected through pitch and intonation. 'Freezing' drops dramatically, with a change in tonal colour over 'red deserts turn to dark', but compared with the extended space explorations of Pink Floyd there is little real innovation. Electronic mixing, the psychedelic coding of distanced sounds, soft explosions and distortion evoke a mood of mystery, of space and being spaced out. Despite the sophistication and beauty, the result is very much that of a studio sound which could have emerged from any space rock stable. Compared with Hendrix, where an immense vocabulary of sound and incredible energy suggested that space exploration ultimately revealed more space[46] *2000 Light Years from Home* returns to interrupted conversations and a voice, remarkably similar to that of Ringo Starr in *Yellow Submarine*.

Interspersed with a parody of *Chopsticks*, the Stones return to a typical theme in an attack on degraded adult pleasures:

> Your wife will never know
> That you're not working late
> Your hostess here is Wendy. . .

Against a constant buzz of 'cocktail' conversation, Jagger, as master of ceremonies, salutes and cautions. Here there is little to suggest his characteristic sense of ego. Rather the assumption of a borrowed voice distances both Jagger and the listener from the song while simultaneously providing a cynical critique of the Beatles' facile view that there is ultimately nothing problematic in relationships that cannot be resolved.[47] So the vocal provides an ironic commentary on the cosy sense of togetherness established in *Yellow Submarine* and the opening chorus of *Sgt. Pepper*. The reference to 'Good evening one and all', 'On with the show' evokes the *Sgt. Pepper* image, but instead of focusing on 'all the lonely people' who can be brought together by love, the Stones reveal a society which hides behind the façade of work ('your wife will never know'), who drink, watch 'cabaret', dance 'gaily round the dance floor' and fight.

In many ways *On with the Show* appears a curious ending to an album entitled *Their Satanic Majesties Request*. The muted understatement is uncharacteristic. There is no feeling of exuberant destruction, which may account for Cohn's opinion that the album is 'boring. . . . It had no rage or arrogance left'.[48] However, while it could be argued that *On with the Show* is unusually deadpan, there is still evidence of Jagger's pessimistic fatalism. The track ends abruptly; there is no magical resolution.

Cohn's dismissal of *Their Satanic Majesties Request* is contentious. There are innovative tracks: *In Another Land,* which demonstrates an ability to mix psychedelic vocabulary with heavy r&b to create the sense of non-reality/reality; the attack on capitalism in *The Citadel* and *On with the Show* and alienation in *2000 Man.* Nevertheless the overall impression of the album is of an ambivalent production. Although more sophisticated than the Stones' preceding albums in terms of orchestration, the complex sound mixes are on the whole ineffectual and confused (the conclusion of side one; the extended raga in *Gomper*). In fact it could be that it is because the orchestration is so obviously *professional* in its studio-based sound that it evokes a feeling of naivety: 'build in extended passages which pull on current psychedelic vocabulary and the result will be contemporary'. It is this lack of authenticity which undermines the authority of the record. The attempt by the Stones to establish an alternative sense of communality based on anarchy and magical exploration lacks thematic conviction, and there is a mismatch between the expectations generated by the cover, the content, style and presentation.

If *Their Satanic Majesties Request* lacked the Stones' usual ferocity, their next album resonated with savagery and it is here that the Stones established their credibility once and for all with the radical branch of the counter-culture.

It may have been an extraordinary chance that whilst the Beatles were releasing their double album *The Beatles*, the Rolling Stones brought out a stranger and more savage record within days. A coincidence, perhaps, but not without irony. While the Beatles sang of *Dear Prudence, Martha My Dear* and *Goodnight Sleep Tight*, the Stones sang of a *Street Fighting Man* itching for bloody revolution.[49]

Street Fighting Man (1968) opens to a heavy r&b beat against a bass riff which extends throughout the verse. The vocal line is similarly repetitive and with Jagger's delivery there is a feeling of relentless force. Following in a tradition of rage and blind anger[50] the song has strong overtones of destruction:

Ev'rywhere I hear the sound of charging feet, oh boy.

'cause summer's here and the time is right for
fighting in the street. . .

The harshness of timbre, the basic aggressiveness of the vocal style and the
bare texture is in marked contrast to *On with the Show*. The slight
hesitation before the 'oh boy' evoke niggling tension, the chance that there
might be a movement towards unbridled aggression. The goading 'But' on
D7 not only effects a change of key, but moves towards a sense of
frustration: 'in sleepy London town, There's just no place for a street
fighting man'. Against a powerful instrumental break, Jagger then screams
out 'No!' before moving into an anarchic 'I'll shout and scream, I'll kill the
king, I'll rail at all his servants'. The setting of London as 'no place for a
street fighting man' provides a stark contrast with their earlier single *We
Love You* which linked the Stones closely with the 'summer of love'. The
bedrock aggression now poses a question: in London, 'what can a poor boy
do except to play for a rock 'n' roll band'?

This question is, to some extent, answered in *Sympathy for the Devil*
(1968). Jagger's anarchic stand is now more universal: 'just call me Lucifer
. . . Or I'll lay your soul to waste.' With Jagger introducing himself as the
Devil, craving for bloody sympathy and interspersed with grunts and
screams, *Sympathy for the Devil* has an effect of 'cold horror and self-
destructive jubilation in which we – through their relentless, pounding,
mocking beat were forcibly being urged to take part'.[51]

Unlike *Street Fighting Man* where Jagger's voice is often obscured by the
density of sound in the backing, *Sympathy for the Devil* makes full use of a
sensuous and fronted delivery. Here the backing is extremely rhythmic,
evoking an ecstatic tribal response with Jagger cast in the role of leader of
the dance. The final coda in particular is jubilant, as Jagger screams out
'what's my name', 'I want ya', 'I want ya baby', 'what's my name?' 'guess my
game', over a heavily vamped accompaniment.

With *Street Fighting Man* and *Beggar's Banquet* the Stones moved back
to their basics and it is here that one can see parallels between the figure of
Jagger, the radical branch of the counter-culture and the psychedelic
satanist Charles Manson who had drifted into Haight-Ashbury in 1967.

Manson had founded a community known as the Family with a structure
of extreme male domination and determined by the equation of sex and
death: 'At once fucking prodigiously, drinking blood, performing ceremo-
nial flailings, robotizing their women into slaves for both sex and murder,
molesting hitch-hikers and acting out sadistic fantasies of all sorts.' Within
the community sexuality and death were unified through the occult, which
allowed for gratuitous and unlimited sex, and lent 'sensuality to the crime in
the ritualisation of murder'.[52]

In his paper 'Charles Manson and the Family', Stuart Ewen argues that
Manson was 'acting out all the myths that societies which are formulated
on unfreedom create about "human nature" without the safeguards of a

controlling authority. If Manson is a rebel he is that ideological rebel that gives substance to counter-revolution.'[53] What separated him from other fact and fiction figures of the period – such as Kissinger or Bond, who were also killers and 'great lovers' – was the fact that Manson was without a job. 'Rather in him we see that dominant culture devoid of its camouflage, stripped of the operational givens of a class society which employ the deformed synthesis of sensuality and violence in the process of social control and production.'[54] 'Thus while it is perfectly reasonable for the American consumer to perform and demand (and, not incidentally, be encouraged in) sex brutality within his consuming unit (i.e. home, family) or when purchasing a sexmodity; sex brutality in the desert is "madness" and "bizarre".'[55]

In many ways the symbolic celebration of the anti-authoritarian figure is embodied in the figure of Mick Jagger, where there is only a thin line between devotion and horror.

> As long as Jagger was merely Satan on stage, the symbolic unity of unmitigated sex-violence was acceptable . . . . When that symbolism began to realise itself in the real social assembly it became horror. Rather than the culture hero representation of sex-violence without bounds, the social practice of the audience began to transcend the symbolic and transmit the utopian into practice. In a cloud of subjects swarming over one another, death and sensuality were united and what they exposed was civilisation in the nascent state.[56]

At Altamont, the hooliganism associated with the Stones' earlier concerts[57] became a fatal certainty when LSD was tied to orgiastic exhibitionism.

> then Mick shouted: 'Hey! Heeey! Hey! Keith – Keith – *Keith*!' By now only Keith was playing, but he was playing as loud and hard as ever, the way the band is supposed to play until the audience tears down the chicken wire and comes on stage with chairs and broken bottles . . . How are we gonna get out of here? I wondered. *Will* we get out, or will we die here? Is it going to snap and the Angels kill themselves and all of us in a savage rage of nihilism, the plain to be found in the morning a bloody soup littered with teeth and bones, one last mad Angel, blinded by a comrade's boots and brass knuckles, gut sliced asunder by his partner's frogsticker, growling, tearing at the yawning slit under his filthy T-shirt, chomping on his own bloody blue white entrails.
> '*Rape, murder, it's just a shot away*', Mick sang over and over.[58]

In the Manson murders there was chaos, 'the wanton commission of violence, somehow ideologically fused with a vision of ungirded sensuality'.[59] In Jagger a parallel position emerges. There was a movement away from the symbolic towards the active, with all its associated horrors. In his music and stage presence there was no longer a symbolic orgy, but a new state of disorder, the extreme edge of freedom which was unleashed at Altamont by his saturnalian presence.

In retrospect it seems likely that the unprecedented and excessive violence was due to the takeover by Hell's Angels, whose policing of the concert was characteristically brutal. Certainly the Stones were initially out of their depth and unable to perform, but as they regained their confidence the harsh explosive sound, together with Jagger's calculated and precise sexuality in the delivery of such songs as *Midnight Rambler* and *Satisfaction*, fed the hysteria in the crowd.[60] The Stones' role at Altamont raises the question of the function of their music. *Midnight Rambler, Satisfaction, Sympathy for the Devil* and *Brown Sugar* express specific insights into society. At one level the songs can be read as a personal view of how society *is*, with the Stones performing the role attributed to artists who provide a window on brutality. In this light the open aggression can be interpreted as taking existing norms so far that they ultimately become unacceptable. Yet the events at Altamont suggest that the songs were interpreted as offering and stimulating an alternative way of life. The stage performance can then be interpreted as both an expression and an active constituent of alternative modes of behaviour – this is *how* you can live.

While the violence at Altamont appears to support the behaviourist argument, the arrogance and brutality in the Stones' music would appear to speak more of the conditions of society. The songs may appear anarchic, but to argue that this necessarily results in destruction is simplistic. It seems more likely that for elements in the counter-culture who were bound up in an aggressive backlash against society the Stones' role as symbolic anarchists was an affirmation of their own position. So while the more cynical could excuse the murder on the grounds that it was 'just one more example of the social norms that inhibit individual freedom', the general reaction among the counter-culture was acute distress. The murder and the Stones' association with Hell's Angels both highlighted the problems of the utopian philosophy of personal freedom and demonstrated how the movement was falling apart at the seams as it attracted the hucksters who fed on the drug culture and the more violent and anarchic elements of the radical underground.

6   Pink Floyd: *Dark Side of the Moon*

Altamont was only one of a series of crises which signalled the demise of the counter-culture. The association of LSD with satanism which had resulted in the Sharon Tate murders[1] resulted in a panic reaction to the adverse effects of drugs. Publicity surrounding the death of famous rock stars also led to highly volatile criticisms of the counter-culture and in particular the concept of creativity through drug experience. In September 1970 Hendrix had been found dead from inhalation of vomit following barbiturate intoxication. On 4 October of the same year, Janis Joplin was dead from a heroin overdose. In 1971 Jim Morrison died of a heart attack caused by heroin or alcohol in Paris. Personal survival seemed paramount and the US broadcast licensing authorities warned radio stations that they would be subverting the government's campaign against drug abuse if they played lyrics which mentioned dope. The bad reception of Joni Mitchell at the Isle of Wight Festival, the disruption of the festival by French, Algerian and American revolutionaries and the questioning of the motives behind Woodstock highlighted the problems of festivals in general. Finally, the killing of four students at Kent State University tragically proved how deep was the gulf between those who wanted to change America and its policies in Vietnam, and the conservative majority who believed in law and order above everything else.

It could be argued that the freeing of rock from its social implications, whether drugs or the wider concerns of fraternity and love, had left music relatively thin in terms of content. The sense of promise that had characterised 1968 dissipated over the next three years as groups generally appeared to lose direction. Some gravitated towards popular music, a trend started by the Beatles in their 1968 *White Album* and exploited in the so-called rock 'n' roll revival and the return of Presley as a live performer. Equally, there was a de-escalation of group consciousness, initially exemplified by the breakup of Cream in 1969. The Beatles' *White Album* also reflects the work of a disintegrating unit, a pastiche of their own past with individual Beatles acting as each other's session men.

Despite the continuing success of such hard r&b groups as the Stones, the rock 'n' roll revival and the emergence of glam rock and reggae in 1970, the music of the early seventies moved towards a more gentle sound which was seen as a reaction to the intensities of mid- to late sixties progressive rock. At the time, theories were put forward for this change in emphasis. The fading of acid rock was seen either as a reflection of the softening of the counter-culture, a tragic slide from activist rage to a mood of enlightened apathy or as progress towards harmony and thoughtfulness as illustrated in the rise of such singer-songwriters as Carole King, Carly Simon and James Taylor. Alternatively it appeared that after the frenzy of such performers as Alice Cooper, Jim Morrison and Arthur Brown rock could only become more gentle. As rock musician Danny Kootch observed in 1970: 'After you set fire to your guitar what do you have left ? Set fire to yourself? It had to go the other way.'[2]

In retrospect, however, the decompression of rock can be traced back to 1968 and Bob Dylan's search for a simpler way of expression, as portrayed in his album *John Wesley Harding*. Among groups, the process was carried to mellow new highs and lows by the Band, whose album *Music from the Big Pink* focused on US rural traditions and folklore with economical playing of the group as a whole. Even groups like Led Zeppelin reflected this shift in direction with the introduction of more semi-acoustic, folk-oriented material, a characteristic which emerges most strongly in *Led Zeppelin IV* (the runes album) with its blend of mysticism and power-driven rock.

Themes explored in Pink Floyd's *Dark Side of the Moon* reflect this shift in direction. The sense of optimism of 1967–8 had passed. Visionary experience and self-discovery had failed to confront the dominant culture, and progressive rock, as part of the counter-culture's revolutionary strategy had, to some extent, stagnated. 'Fraternal individualism' had metamorphosed into elitist exhibitonism; the thinking behind unpredictable extended forms of music had been turned into LP-length easy listening; psychedelic sound had become isolated from innovative developments in harmony, rhythm and electronics to become fetishised, detached from radical implications. While this could in part be attributed to the breakup of key groups, the deaths of Hendrix, Morrison and Joplin and the growing belief in individualism, it was inevitable that music should move in a new direction, one more in tune with the economic and social conditions of the early seventies – poverty and the dole queue, petty crime, high-rise living, street violence and boredom.

Dark Side of the Moon occupies a position similar to that of *Sgt. Pepper* as a symbolic point in the history of rock. Both the Beatles and Pink Floyd explore contemporary problems, but whereas *Sgt. Pepper* reflects the heady optimism of 1967, its extended exploration of the psychedelic reflecting the counter-culture's belief, 'change the mode of consciousness and you change the world', Pink Floyd seem to close the book. Work, money, growing old, going mad are expressed through a song cycle which begins and ends with a fading heartbeat.

The cover of *Dark Side of the Moon* contains no words, just a prism with a shaft of white light on one side emerging split into the colours of the spectrum on the other, set against a black background. Obviously there is a marketing function: the cover has enigmatic appeal, it is a collector's item, but there is also a link between the image on the cover, the image of the group and the music itself.

Floyd's obsession with electronic sound and light shows is signified by the breaking down of white light by the prism, a scientific process that evokes the image of a high-technology group. Aesthetically, the image can be seen as a literal signifier of the psychedelic effect that Floyd hoped to achieve through the fusion of sound with light. At a deeper level, it can be interpreted as inspiration (clear white light) converted through musical and technological transformation (the prism) into the psychedelic range of sound and meaning (the whole spectrum). So the image encapsulates not only the philosophy of the group but also the philosophy of the counter-culture itself with its emphasis on alternative structures of meaning.

The link between the cover and the overall style of production is also interesting. Taped effects and synthesisers are used extensively and it is a highly technical production. In the late sixties and early seventies, progressive rock had incorporated techniques from such avant-garde composers as Stockhausen, Cage, Satie, Messiaen, Varèse and Stravinsky. On the continent, bands such as Burning Red Ivanhoe, Magma and Amon Duul II had concentrated on technically complex playing, electronics and studio effects, acknowledging their debt to both twentieth-century classical composers and those bands who had espoused 'improvisation' with 'electronics': Grateful Dead, Jefferson Airplane, Soft Machine, Cream and Pink Floyd. The cover of *Dark Side of the Moon* may be an acknowledgement of this shared interest in innovatory technology.

In *Dark Side of the Moon*, the linking of technology to its more threatening aspect in *Us and Them* is to some extent analagous with Penderecki's *Threnody to the Victims of Hiroshima* and to the Beatles' *A Day in the Life* where synthesised sound is used to create an hallucinogenic nightmare. This linking of electronic sound to threatening situations was not new. In *Take up Thy Stethoscope and Walk*, on Pink Floyd's first album for example, humanity is operated on by horrific electronic and brain-battering noises to evoke a terrifyingly realistic medical allegory.

Overall, then, the cover of *Dark Side of the Moon* suggests a highly produced album, both technologically and artistically, which refers to past precedents and contemporary trends in progressive rock.

There are five major tracks on each side of the album, all of which are linked musically and conceptually to contribute towards a cyclical effect, with the record opening and closing with a sound resembling the pumping of the human heart, the fundamental signifier of life.

The opening track is a montage of bizarre sound images and taped emotions which create an often disembodied, hallucinatory impression of the threat of madness.[3] Just as surrealistic art speaks directly to individualised secret fears and emotions through universal signifiers, so the juxtaposition of images on this track creates an experience of madness. As individual pulses conform to a common rate under the stimulus of an amplified heart, so the opening ten seconds cause the listener to move towards the communality of pace necessary to shared experience.

The pulse rate established, *Speak to Me* moves through images of time and madness: the superimposed ticking clock, signifier of passing time and the manic 'I've been mad for fucking years, absolutely years, over the edge . . .' – the voice of Pink Floyd's roadie, Roger the Hat, committed to the experience of the group, linked to the Floyd's earlier exploration of the psychedelic. The sound of the till ties madness to the material world and the written image; the reiterated 'I've always been mad' reinforces the dominant theme with the technology of the helicopter, itself juxtaposed with screams of insanity which slowly subside into the first chord of *Breathe*.

The first track suggests 'head' music, introspective and with the emphasis on the heightened awareness central to counter-cultural ideology. Madness/ alienation/technology and its attendant miseries are established as the primary themes informing the album, with the sound and imagery being sufficiently text-related to provide a strong indication of a preferred reading, madness and man's inhumanity as signified by capitalism and technology.

The sweetly tonal construction of the following track, *Breathe*, with its almost innocent use of triadic harmony, achieves an instantaneous change of mood. There is a naivety in sound and a sense of beauty which seem to indicate a rebirth of harmony out of the chaos of the preceding track. The gentle pulse evokes the sense of a new order, which is enhanced by electronic distancing to create a spatial dimension comparable to that experienced on a trip. This evocation of the psychedelic is also reflected in the chord structures. What seem to be straightforward harmonies (Em–A) are subtly modified by added ninths to suggest an inner ambiguity. Without the overt pessimism of the words, *Breathe* could convey a quiet retreat into a hallucinatory unknown.

The question arises of why there is this apparent contrast in mood between an escapist dream-like world – suggested by the attenuated and subtly changed chords, the pitch distortions, the filtering and the lazy vocal tone – and the predictability and limitations of reality as established by the lyrics in the first verse ('smiles you'll give and tears you'll cry') and the parameters of known existence ('All you touch and all you see is all your life will ever be').

The mood established by the music is illusory. Life *is* predictable in its race to an early grave and at best the seductiveness of the drug-induced states created by the music can provide only a false sense of security. The sweetly tonal melody, the gently floating pulse disguise the threat, lulling the listener into a state of illusion/delusion. It is possible to drift through life as imaged in the constant floating chords and pulse, but there is no escape from its transitory nature or from the accumulating tempo of work, the survival tactics which depend on going with society, but which still drive 't'ward an early grave', as suggested by the downward shape of the final three chords.

In the second verse in particular, the lyrics work against the dreamlike harmonies and scoring. The *other way*, as implied by the continuity of the music, remains, but it is no more than hallucination and should be read along with the realism of the lyrics. 'Run, run rabbit, run' is still sung with the same lazy intonation, there is no change in pulse, the chords continue as before, floating and dreamy, but the treadmill nature of life is unchallengeable. Again the calmness of the music may seduce the listener into security, but it is an illusion:

> balanced on the biggest wave
> You race t'wards an early grave.

It is possible to 'fly high', to blow one's mind, but there can be no escape. Within the total context of the album, escape can only lead to *The Dark Side of the Moon*, and as the last chord dies away, *On The Run* re-establishes paranoia, running on the spot, as signified by the ostinato, which as a formal device can at best provide only an illusion of progress, its perpetual state of motion signifying the relentless movement of life.[4] It is not surprising that with the concept of a 'race towards an early grave' established, the idea should be taken over by a bricolage of sound effects related to travel and movement: the disembodied, anonymous voice on the airport lounge tannoy, the response of pounding footsteps going nowhere; the slow crescendo of synthesised helicopter rotors over a temporarily reversed ostinato; the reinstatement of the ostinato motif over a repeated rotor sound; an indistinct 'Live for today, go for tomorrow' followed by a staccato laugh; a train entering a tunnel followed by another gradual crescendo of sound leading to variations on the ostinato; a manic laugh and a crash which slowly fades into the ticking of a clock, thus linking *On the Run* both to the concept of the madness of material existence initially established in *Speak to Me* and to the next track, *Time*.

Lyrically, *Breathe* and *Time* are linked. Both deal with society positioning the individual for its own use, and gradually taking over his/her entire life:

> Run, rabbit run
> Dig that hole, forget the sun
> Then at last, the work is done
> Don't sit down, it's time to dig another one.
>
> (*Breathe*)

> And you run and you run to catch up with the sun but it's sinking
> Racing around to come up behind you again.

The sun is the same in a relative way, but you're older
Shorter of breath and one day closer to death.

(*Time*)

Time opens with a jarring, multi-chime effect, alarm clocks, striking clocks, peals, strident reminders of time's morning domination. A gradual fade on the sixth stroke leads to the semiquaver beat of the tom-toms establishing the basic pulse over which the heavy E major/F minor chords ride slowly on a two-bar alternating harmony.

At the same time, a synthesised xylophone effect plays an off-beat counterpoint to the variedly syncopated rhythms of the tom-toms. As in *Breathe*, the twenty-four-bar introduction creates a space and expansiveness after the frenzied activity of the preceding sound collage. The effect is to highlight the dominance of time, its strength and sense of unity achieved by the strength of the pedantic alternating chords of E major/F minor. Time is in control, man is on the run; this is established both by the preceding track and by the song itself, which deals with the unequal race of survival, the seemingly endless years of youth which suddenly catch up, leaving the individual 'hanging on in quiet desperation'.

The song is in two contrasting sections on an ABAB pattern. Verses one and three have a narrow-ranged repetitive melody which, in conjunction with the rhythmic pulse, creates a feeling of controlled movement. This is enhanced by a certain mechanical quality in the rhythmic patterning and regularity of the lines. There is an impression of time 'ticking away', the accenting both propelling the melody forward and focusing on the key words that inform the meaning of the song:

Ticking away the moments that make up a dull day

Fritter and waste the hours in an off-hand way

In contrast, the musical expansiveness of verses two and four create a more lazy mood, the melody moves slowly over gently shifting harmonies to create a deceptive timelessness:

You are young and life is long and there is time to kill today

This is enhanced by the more relaxed delivery of the male vocalist and the subtle echo effects of the female duetting. There is a warm, laid-back quality in the delivery that creates a mood of eternal summer, the 'oooooh-aaaaah' harmonising of the duetting creating a relaxed sense of well-being as it gently reinforces the alternating D–A harmonies which support the vocal line. In context, however, the lyrics seem an ironic commentary on the inability of man to come to terms with the accelerating pace of time. As the second verse ends, a guitar solo takes over to evoke the space-dream atmosphere associated with post-*Gnome*, a track on Pink Floyd's *Piper at the Gates of Dawn*.

So the relaxed mood of *Time* creates a false security. There are subtle links with *Breathe*, where there is a similarly constructed sense of timelessness through the simple alternation of the two-chord structure. The melody of *Time* is a subtle variation on the *Breathe* theme, and the warmth and sense of safety is shadowed by the tension created by the dissonant harmonies, the circumscribed nature of life and the quiet desperation of hanging on:

All you touch and all you see is all your life will ever be!

(*Breathe*)

Hanging on in quiet desperation

(*Time*)

The melody line of verses two and four of *Time* are also similar to *Breathe* in their narrow range, the sequential structure reinforcing the theme of the repetitive nature of time, the inevitability of the sun 'sinking and racing round to come up behind you again . . . but you're older . . . one day closer to death' (verse 3).

The gentle pulse in verses two and four may suggest a slowness evocative of a trip, with the phrases hypnotically repeated to create a mood of fixation, but it is this very state of mind that allows time to win in the end. Unprepared, we find that 'the time is gone, the song is over'.

The bending of the notes, the reverberation and the duetting of the guitar with the 'heavenly choir' create the idea of man disappearing into the vastness of space. Electronic distancing, the lazy 'vocal' tone of the guitar, the hallucinatory timbres work together to create a sweetly tonal construction. Time can only win in the end, and the more expansive the sense of time, the smaller man becomes in comparison, the more certain his ultimate devastation.

From the quiet desperation of *Time*, the album moves into a reprise of *Breathe* on an appropriately plagal cadence that musically establishes the home/church-centred theme. Here images of safety – fireside, tolling church bells – are pulled into association. The iron bell, eternal, measured and controlled by man

Calls the faithful to their knees
To hear the softly spoken magic spells

before sinking into the opening piano chords of *The Great Gig in the Sky*.

Nothing could be more perfectly peaceful and hymn-like than the opening chords of this track. Its clear, simple texture and structure has a solemn Lutheran quality that recalls the rebirth of order, humanity and beauty more typical of the cosmic music of Pink Floyd.[5] There are two dominant moods: the first a sense of childlike wonder and naivety; the second an orgasmic high. Both are achieved through the explicit but enigmatically emotional singing of Clare Torry.

Overall the timbre of the male vocal on both *Breathe* and *Time* is smooth and even, almost texturally bland, providing an unemotional commentary on the time-dominated measure of life. In contrast, the female voice is allowed a different expression, soaring without words, often like a primeval scream.

The song is preceded by the male spoken statement, which sets the mood:

Why should I be frightened of dying?
There's no reason for it, you've got to go sometime.

This is echoed in the female vocalist's whispered reply near the end of the song:

I never said I was afraid of dying.

There is a certain feeling of cliché, but the matter-of-fact male delivery heightens the bluesy female voice, which works like an unspoken philosophical musing, conveying agony, fear, anger, orgasmic high before the expression of childlike wonder when the harmonies return to their opening sequence. Her 'was very good tonight' highlights and contrasts the freedom of sexual and psychedelic release with the preceding death theme of mechanical domination in *Breathe* and *Time* – a mood which also emerges in *Money*.

Money is both pivotal and oppositional. Its key position (first track, side two) locates the song both within the album itself (*Great Gig in the Sky*, hallucinogenic withdrawal; *Us and Them*, oppositions) and re-establishes the primary theme, contemporary society's threats and disillusionment, its pressures and hypercritical values which can ultimately lead to madness. Unlike *Within You Without You* – the pivotal track on the *Sgt. Pepper* Album, which investigates Eastern mysticism and its potential for the counter-cultural movement through a rejection of the ego-centricity of Western civilisation – *Money* attacks.

By 1973 it had become apparent that counter-cultural 'gut solidarity . . . common aspirations, inspirations, strategy, style and mood'[6] had not been sufficient to change society. The freedom to question and experiment implicit in the counter-culture's ideological and cultural protest was both fragmented and had

> diverted attention away from the structural inequalities of capitalist society: by criticising technology rather than the property-owning rich, by demanding quality in life rather than the satisfaction of basic needs and by elevating youth disaffiliation as the motor of social change rather than class conflict and struggle.[7]

To retreat into Eastern mysticism, to rely on drugs, to drop out may have appeared a positive alternative to the repressive processes of society in 1967–8,[8] but later it became obvious that hippie culture had become translated into a commercial ideology. As Frith points out: 'Rock musicians' culture as a whole is not really much different from that of any other group of entertainers: their object is to give a particular market what it wants.[9] Hendrix had received £100,000 for his appearance at Newport in 1969 having played free at his first festival. Other super-groups were constant performers on the US festival circuit: the Stones, The Who, Jeff Beck and Procol Harum received particularly exorbitant fees and the history of rock festivals throughout the 1970s was increasingly characterised by com-mercialisation.

Money speaks of the hypocrisy by which values are traduced and the way in which the person is denied in favour of extrapersonal goals:

> New car, caviar, four-star daydream
> Think I'll buy me a football team

and yet ironically, this has been the most successful track of the album, a continually revived classic with cover versions by at least three other singers and bands. However, while *Money*'s commercial appeal is reiterated in the theme of the song, it still functions politically by focusing attention both on the inequalities of a capitalist society and through the ambiguities of the word stash itself, with its drug connotations.

> But if you ask for a rise
> It's no surprise that they're giving none away (verse 3).
> Money, it's a gas
> Grab that cash with both hands and make a stash (verse 1).

The success of the track, both as a single and within the album, lies in its breezy authoritative incisiveness. It is no 'message song' in the tradition of Lennon's *Power to the People* or *Give Peace a Chance*, but a robustly ironic comment on capitalism. The coolly sophisticated music meshes with the words into a lively social commentary which is all-inclusive. None of us is free from this social disease, the sentiments are universal:

> Share it fairly
> But don't take a slice of my pie.

The relentless precision of the bass guitar riff in the introduction is a musical analogy of a businesslike approach to the acquisition of wealth. Simulta-neously the subtle alternating 3/4, 4/4 metres and lead guitar motif convey a quiet acquiescence, as the listener is lulled into a false sense of safety: 'Money, it's a gas!'

The alternating major/minor harmonies, which continue throughout the verse, move towards a sense of tension/release/tension:

Money	Ya get a- way,	ya
Bm7	E/D Bm7	E/D
get a good job with more pay and		you're O.-K.
Bm7		E/D Bm7

This is reinforced by the downward movement and melisma over key words such as 'O–K', working towards a disillusionment which is fed by the downward shape of the vocal line on 'Money'. While instructions 'Get a good job with more pay', 'Grab that cash with both hands' are sung out in strong, punchy crotchets the sense of personal inability to control is still there. The cash may be in your hands (to a rising motif) but at best you 'make a stash' (downwards and resolved on Bm7).

The strongly physical quality in the overlay of rhythmic till sounds and money in verses two and three conveys the mechanisation of life. At the same time, the illusory power of money is confirmed in the declamatory section at the end of each verse. Here the metre shifts between $\frac{3}{4}$, $\frac{5}{4}$ with a stop time deflection on the penultimate note. The effect is to stress both the power of purchase:

> Think I'll buy me a football . . . . team
> I think I need a Lear . . . . Jet

and the hypocrisy underlying the concept of 'fair share':

> but don't take a slice of my . . . . pie

In some ways, this reads as Floyd's recognition of new realism. The counter-culture had attempted to set up alternative life styles based on communal living which were expressed as a negation of the dominant culture. As an early British underground band, whose increasing popularity had brought both prestige and money, Pink Floyd have a certain tongue-in-cheek recognition of their position within the wider capitalist context in which their music was produced and distributed. This reading appears to be confirmed in the last verse's wry and unequivocal statement: 'They're giving none away.' Here there are no delay tactics and the sense of finality is given added emphasis through repetition.

Then, over a fading riff and vocal duetting on the theme, Waters comments, often inaudibly, on the savagery and violence of a materialistic society by evoking the atmosphere of a police inquiry:

> 'I certainly was in the right'
> 'I was really drunk at the time'
> 'Did anybody do anything?'
> 'Cruising for bruising'

The words resonate with the law and order politics of the time. So the sardonic lyrics are developed into a form of political intrigue, an enigmatic thread which pulls the listener into the dialogue, but one which leaves the lines open-ended, for the audience alone can fill in the answers.

Money exposes the sickness of Western culture through an ironic and humorous approach. The pretentiousness of owning other people: 'Think I'll buy me a football team', for example, is attacked with a suitably open and unpretentious musical style which echoes the underlying ethos of rock: to liberate anything that has been oppressed. *Money* thus becomes the energy centre of *Dark Side of the Moon*. It articulates the problems of a materialistic society in straightforward language and in doing so mirrors the frustrations of its audience, who in turn can reflect on their dissatisfaction with society and the problems that drive people apart. There is no sense of social reconstruction (as experienced, for example, in *Within You Without You*) and it is soon apparent that the track simply prepares its audience for the tragic oppositions of *Us and Them* and the redefinition of madness in *Brain Damage*. As a single its success may have been commercial: in the context of the album it is political, reflecting Pink Floyd's belief that 'their music should be useful to the living. For to live amongst the living is to care.'[10]

With 'I was really drunk at the time' providing a last comment on the purchasing power – and outcome – of money, there emerges a sustained D major chord on the organ which is slowly overlaid by the opening chords of *Us and Them*.

If *Money* was a specific attack on materialism, *Us and Them* reflects disillusion with modern society in general. The attack is subtle and effected through two juxtaposed styles, the first gentle and reflective highlighting oppositions:

'Us and Them'
'Me and You'
'Black and Blue'
'Up and Down'
'Down and Out'

the second, more aggressive and didactic, singling out war and man's inhumanity to man for special consideration.[11]

The mood of the first verse is established in the introduction, which is based on a ten-bar riff that poignantly conveys the unchanging reality of life. The chords move gently from D major, through Bm/D to Dm7 back to D major via G/D to create an arch shape.

The melodic riff is simultaneously supported and anticipated by the rising structure of the top note of the guitar chords. The movement between D major and D minor creates an underlying tension whilst the constant root movement between D and A provides stability through repetition which counters any progressive implications.[12] The effect is of serenity and this is enhanced when the ten bars are repeated with a smooth sax improvisation, itself anticipating and reflecting on the ensuing melodic line of the first verse.

At this point the meaning of the song is ambivalent and its gently floating character could equally well provide a route to hallucinogenic escape: the surface conventions of psychedelic style are present in the electronic distortion, the bright hallucinary timbres and the lazy delivery of the sax line.

The melodic line of the verse is gentle too; its relaxed phrasing is enhanced by echo effects which form a sensual overlay of sound above the guitar riff. The harmonies are also straightforward, the vocal line almost naive in its simplicity. Above all, there is a lack of display which, in conjunction with the words, creates a sense of honesty in the seemingly calm attack on the oppositions in society: 'Us and Them'.

Yet this can also be interpreted as mirroring our own laid-back attitude towards countering inequalities. Lulled by the riff, it is only too easy to miss the tensions (connoted by the added sevenths and ninths) and the fact that 'after all, we're only ordinary men', that life is 'up and down'.

Us and Them shows us an alternative approach to life. *Time* reflected on the inevitability of movement towards death; *Us and Them* revealed life's lack of progress: it moves up and down, but in the end movement is an illusion. Like the continuous riff, there is no real progression:

> Black and blue
> And who knows which is which
> And who is who

The verses are simply reflective, identifying the polarities that drive people apart, the underlying futility and inability to move or to change society.

In contrast to the verse, the chorus's powerful narratives highlight specific inequalities in society: the General who orders the front rank forward, the myth of the 'battle of words', the failure to provide for the needy, contrasts of rank, power and wealth which result in poverty and death. This time Floyd draw on the anti-war philosophy of the counter-culture and the fears of manipulation which were to appear later in *The Wall*'s terrifying insights into man's inhumanity to man:

> Forward he cried from the rear
> And the front rank died.
> The General sat
> And the lines on the map moved from side to side.

(Us and Them)

Again the sentiments are expressed through a clear, simple texture with a use of triadic harmony to recreate a mood of childlike wonder at the senselessness of destruction. Yet the innocence is constructed and there are similarities in the simplicity of compositional approach to Lennon and McCartney's *A Day in the Life*, which also explores the mundane and the predictable, but which releases it to the bizarre and the exotic rather than highlighting and opposing war and social inequality. Even so, the outcome of both tracks is similar. Both end ultimately in madness: for Lennon it is a hallucinogenic nightmare, for Waters *Brain Damage* and the pressures that lead to insanity.

The break is psychedelic rock in the true Pink Floyd tradition, providing a reservoir of sound and improvisation which allows the listener to experience without the pain connected with word-consciousness, to reach new psychic worlds and so escape the old. However, unlike earlier compositions such as *Interstellar Overdrive* where disordered, apparently randomised electronically dominated noise prevails, or *Saucerful of Secrets* where only occasional drumbeats intrude upon the general chaos, the instrumental postlude to *Us and Them*, aptly described as *Any Colour You Like*, has both structure and a sense of beauty. The underlying harmonies provide a certain rationality which hints at control, and while the unpleasantness of contemporary society is drowned in a psychedelic, space-rock sound, there is no simple conclusion that this track is yet another example of 'shutting your eyes and blowing your mind'. Instead there is mutual influence, a harmonic structuring of the improvisation, giving the seemingly floating, free-form solo a basic strength. *Any Colour You Like* could indicate an alternative to the artificiality and dishonesty of the materialistic world identified in the two preceding tracks. At the same time, as the shimmering sounds subside into the more earth-bound D major ostinato of *Brain Damage*, there is an indication that only the strong will continue to survive, that psychedelic release is only temporary and can lead to madness or death.[13]

The threat of madness is omnipresent in *Brain Damage*, but as Pink Floyd ask, *who* defines it?

> You rearrange me till I'm sane
> You lock the door
> And throw away the key
> There's someone in my head, but it's not me.

The underlying riff in *Brain Damage* informs, with only minor modifications, the whole verse structure of the track. In this it images psychotic art in general where repetitions of small motifs continue, often without the slightest change, for the duration of a patient's life. *Brain Damage* is consistent both in its insistence on simplicity of motif and its recognition of the hostility to the subject's position: 'Got to keep the loonies on the path.'

The vocal line is narrow ranged, the accent displaced, subconsciously reflecting the positioning of the lunatic within society. The simple movement from # to ♮ underlines the poignancy of the words, gentle and natural images of childhood, daisy chains and grass contrasting with the inhumanity of the materialistic world identified on earlier tracks. For society, the lunatic is often a feared deviant, and the hostile response is unequivocal and on the beat with the added seventh suggesting an eternity of tension before the gentle reassertion of the D-major riff. There is also a tacit acknowledgement that madness is all-pervasive: the pressures of society can engender madness. Singular moves to plural, impersonal to personal: 'The lunatic is in the hall, the lunatics are in *my* hall'.

The media identify the ever-increasing numbers:

> The paper holds their folded faces to the floor,

And every day the paper boy brings more.

So there is a sting in the tail of the lyrics. The real madmen are not the ones you label as mad, but the politicians on the front pages of the morning papers.

The music then moves into an assertive G major as the chorus identifies the inevitable consequences of social pressures. The duetting on the vocal line is in strong parallel thirds, with a vocal backing suggesting a negro-spiritual choir, and this is supported by strong chords on the guitar. Again the movement is minimal but the higher register identifies the intensity of the emotion, the underlying panic. The reiterated words, 'And if, And if, And if', do not spell out a real possibility. Instead they push towards the inevitability of darkness and madness, the dark forebodings in the head linked to the *Dark Side of the Moon* before the despairing wail of recognition that 'the lunatic is in my head', which is supported by superimposed manic laughter. Ultimately, society has the say in who is sane, who is the lunatic.

The final chorus draws heavily on Syd Barrett's breakdown, providing authenticity for the overwhelming pessimism of the track – 'if only they [EMI] could have seen Syd standing on stage drooling and playing the same chord all evening'[14] – Here there is a subtle change in rhythmic emphasis from the last chorus as if to underline Syd's lack of co-ordination – 'And if the band you're in starts playing a diff'rent tune. . .'. The final line, however, remains. The dark side of the moon does not change, it is omnipresent. The muttering of Roger the Hat's response to death – 'It's one of those things that never goes out of fashion' – and his stoned laughter create a mood of genuine despair before the mind is gently lulled by the fading ostinato and the dreamy introduction to *Eclipse*.

Eclipse is almost religious in its incantatory repetition of the vocal line. The quasi-liturgical lyrics with their blues backing and simple arpeggiated accompaniment suggest naivety, a return to a state of peace. This is confirmed by the finality of the V–I cadence supporting the vocal line 'and everything under the sun is in tune'. Yet it appears that there is to be no such reprieve; the music moves towards a final plagal cadence, an almost hymn-line effect.

The final track points to the fallacy of escape from madness. Initially it may appear that psychedelic escape is preferable to mechanistic social pressures but the lyrics indicate that both paths lead in the same inevitable direction. As the song points out : 'everything under the sun is in tune but the sun is eclipsed by the moon.' As the moon is traditionally associated with lunacy, everything ultimately ends in madness.

The mocking laughter is, then, against society in general:

There's no Dark Side of the Moon really.
Matter of fact it's all dark

and this idea is linked to the final heartbeat. Life goes on and the album, with its mixture of materialism and madness, has come the full circle. The concept is complete.

Floyd's involvement with film scores (*Come in Number 51, Your Time Is Up*, December 1969; *Zabriskie Point*, 1969; *The Body*, 1970; and *Obscured By Clouds*, 1972) may account for the clarity and impression of graphic continuity experienced when listening to *Dark Side of the Moon*. The words act like dialogue over the music, impressionistic yet making a point. As the album deals with stress, lunacy and death in contemporary society, so the disembodied vocal timbres create effective commentary: cynical asides and taped effects underline the inhuman quality still further by creating an abstract collage against which to project the emptiness of modern life; while the electronic treatment of instrumental and vocal sounds helps to reinforce the distancing of space as signified through pure tone, electronically synthesised.

Even so, the album can be considered somewhat of an enigma as far as the counter-culture itself is concerned. The focus on money, for example, can be interpreted as an attack on mainstream culture, but at the same time it highlights one of the paradoxes facing the counter-culture in its ultimate reliance on capital.

Hippies were disdainful of capitalist enterprise, yet gave birth to numerous small capitalist businesses in T-shirts, pop art, posters, underground newspapers and drug-related paraphernalia. Their creation and appropriation of style also gave renewed life to established consumer industries. In 1969, the CBS record company found the perfect marketing strategy by claiming that it was dedicated to promoting the 'revolutionaries', and the Woodstock Music and Arts Festival was eagerly commercialised by Warner Brothers who gained filming rights and Atlantic who secured recording rights. By reworking the old themes of peace and love, record companies created many artists whose sole purpose was to imitate the music of the counter-culture to fill the bestselling charts.[15]

It is possible that *Dark Side of the Moon* is a musical attempt to work through and come to terms with success, not just the success of Pink Floyd and other progressive rock bands, but also of the people buying the record. It can be seen as a warning to those who are having to come to terms with money, commuting, who are already *on the run*, the tacit recognition that the counter-culture itself was equally dependent on money and capitalism, not least to support its dependence on drugs.

At the same time there is a continuing focus on the psychedelic. Repressive affluence, technological domination, individual conformity and materialism, which had been identified by Roszak as endemic in contemporary society,[16] are musically encoded as mindless and auto-destructive (e.g. the overlay of effects in *On The Run* and *Time*) and are juxtaposed with subjectivity (*Breathe*) dissociation and individualism (*The Great Gig in the*

Sky) in hallucinogenic tracks conveying psychedelic experience. The focus on madness, however, encodes caution. The investigation of the pressures of living in a technological society can lead to *Brain Damage* or possible release through LSD (*The Great Gig in the Sky, Any Colour You Like*) but the album is also a sometimes implicit, sometimes explicit condemnation of drugs as a route to personal freedom: 'All that you give, all that you deal, all that you buy, beg borrow or steal . . . is eclipsed by the moon' (*Eclipse*); 'For long you live and high you fly, but only if you ride the tide, and balanced on the biggest wave, you race toward an early grave' (*Breathe*). The gentle pulse and timelessness in *Breathe* may suggest a retreat into the beauty of an hallucinatory unknown, but the lyrics imply caution. Life is predictable in its race to an early grave and at best the seductiveness of the drug-induced state suggested by the music can only provide a false security. The differences in mood in *Time* also encode a similar sense of the illusory nature of escape and the cyclical form of *Us and Them*, despite its overt attack on society, hints at the problems caused by LSD, emphasising the need for support. Even the seemingly free improvisation of the female voice in *Great Gig in the Sky* is underpinned by structured harmonies, again implying a need for release anchored by stability.

There is a suggestion that while the need for freedom still exists, the cult of psychedelia which was inscribed within counter-cultural consciousness as a means of broadening personal experience, the philosophy of 'Feed your head and blow your mind' was inadequate. Political and social confrontation had become fragmented; subjective experience had degenerated into *play power*, which had little purchase other than an irreverent and often irrelevant questioning of authority, materialism and capitalism. The album criticises both mainstream society and the counter-culture. Unlike earlier albums, *Dark Side of the Moon* does not celebrate LSD, for the beauty of escape is often contrasted with its attendant evils: 'I've been mad for fucking years, absolutely years, over the edge . . .'. *Time* and *Money* attack society, capitalism, technology, *Brain Damage* defines the madness that can ensue from its attendant pressures, but *Eclipse* encodes the final paradigm, the dark side of the moon, its possible beauty, but nevertheless its other-worldliness.

Notes

1. INTRODUCTION

1 R. Levin, 'Rock and Regression: The Responsibility of the Artist', in J. Sinclair, and R. Love, *Music and Politics*, New York, 1971, 131.

2. T. Roszak, *The Making of a Counter Culture: Reflections on the Technocratic Society and its Youthful Opposition*, Faber & Faber, 1971, 156.

3. R. Neville, *Play Power*, Paladin, 1971, 14.

4. Ibid.

5. Roszak, op. cit., 2.

6. Ibid, 56.

7. Ibid, 64.

8. Psychedelic (acid) rock had first emerged in the summer of 1965 in the Red Dog Saloon in Nevada. Pioneered by the Charlatans, the fusion of rock 'n' roll, crude light shows and LSD laid the foundation for what was to be known as the 'frisco scene. Initially centred at the Longshoreman's Hall, and fronted by Chet Helms of the Family Dog, the alliance of loud, improvised music with dance and LSD attracted a cult audience drawn from a growing hippy community. By late 1965 two venues had been established: the Avalon Ballroom under Chet Helms and the Fillmore under the promotion of Bill Graham.

   It would be misleading, however, to suggest that acid rock was a single musical phenomenon and while dance was a critical aspect of the 'frisco scene, the emergence of such groups as Jefferson Airplane, the Warlocks (subsequently the Grateful Dead) and Big Brother and the Holding Company, established an alliance with the California folk movement. Musicians were equally attracted to San Francisco from Los Angeles (Love, Kaleidoscope and the Leaves), Texas (Steve Miller) and the East Coast (Paul Butterfield's Blues Band, Lovin' Spoonful and the Blues Project). At the same time, San Francisco saw the emergence of such groups as Country Joe and the Fish, Moby Grape and the Quicksilver Messenger Service.

   The 'frisco scene was at its peak in 1966 and its demise is largely attributable to exploitation by the media, promoters and record companies. Essentially it had been held together by a sense of inner cohesion and while there was a musical diversity of style, the emphasis on free expression had resulted in a rock vocabulary which focused acid experience. The publicity surrounding the hippy community may have resulted in the spread of counter-cultural ideology (e.g. an emphasis on love and acid) but the identification of San Francisco, as a centre for creativity and innovation was, in retrospect, short-lived.

9. Neville, op. cit., 79.

10. See P. E. Willis, *Profane Culture,* Routledge & Kegan Paul, London, 1978.
11. J. Fort, *The Pleasure Seekers: The Drug Crisis, Youth and Society*, Grove Press, New York, 1969.
12. R. Middleton and J. Muncie, 'Pop Culture, Pop Music and Post-war Youth: Counter-cultures', in *Popular Culture,* Open University Press, Milton Keynes, 1981, 87.

2 CREAM, HENDRIX AND PINK FLOYD

1. K. Emerson, 'Britain: The Second Wave', in *Rolling Stone Illustrated History of Rock and Roll*, Random House, New York, 1976, 282.
2. D. Downing, *Future Rock*, Panther, St Albans, 1976, 107.
3. *Melody Maker*, June 1967.
4. Downing, op. cit., 107.
5. R. Neville, *Play Power*, Paladin, London, 1971, 79.
6. R. Middleton and J. Muncie, 'Pop Culture, Pop Music and Post-war Youth: Counter-cultures', in *Popular Culture*, Open University Press, Milton Keynes, 1981, 79.
7. Ibid., 778.
8. Clapton: 'First group, The Roosters Jan–Sept 1963, early British R&B outfit also featuring Tom McGuiness. Occasional appearances with Blues Inc. at Ealing, London as "stand in" for Mick Jagger. With McGuiness spent two weeks in October 1963 with Casey Jones and the Engineers before replacing Anthony "Top" Topham in Yardbirds as lead guitarist.

   Was with Yardbirds up to group's March '65 *For Your Love* hit single but left soon after . . . Worked short while on building site until offer to join John Mayall's Bluesbreakers, spring '65 . . .

   Recorded on number of albums with Mayall before handing over guitar spot to Peter Green July 1966 and forming Cream with Jack Bruce and Ginger Baker.

   Bruce: At 17 won scholarship to Royal Scottish Academy of Music. First gained attention playing R&B on double bass in Graham Bond Organisation, subsequently appeared in John Mayall's Bluesbreakers and Manfred Mann before founding Cream with Baker and Clapton.

   Baker: Played in a number of jazz bands including those led by British trad jazzers Acker Bilk and Terry Lightfoot, before replacing Charlie Watts in Alexis Korner's Blues Incorporated in 1962.

   Left Blues Inc in February following year with Graham Bond and Jack Bruce to form Graham Bond Trio – later Graham Bond Organisation – and remained with Bond for more than three years before forming Cream with Clapton and Bruce. (N. Logan and B. Wooffinden, *The Illustrated Encyclopedia of Rock*, Salamander Books, London, 1976, 54, 44, 18).
9. Middleton and Muncie, op. cit., 80.
10. This analysis, and others by Cream, can be followed by reference to Pearce Marchbank, *Cream*, Wise Publications, London, 1977.
11. In the sense of a denotational relationship to the physical experience characteristic of hallucinatory conditions. 'In particular the main dimensions of LSD reaction are perceptual, cognitive (thought) and affective (mood). . . . With the eyes open, a particular object, painting or leaf that would not ordinarily be seen in the forest will receive considerable attention extending over a period of many minutes. As an example, one may see subtle undulations of the configuration of the leaf and many variations in the shades of greenness that would ordinarily not be apprehended . . . Ordinary boundaries and controls between the self and the

environment and within the self are loosened.' (J. Fort, *The Pleasure Seekers: The Drug Crisis, Youth and Society*, Grove Press, New York, 1969, 182).

In the song, the repetition works against the expectations generated by the traditional use of cadences and in conjunction with the words moves towards a perceptual change analogous to that associated with LSD.

12. Woman tone is associated with timbre and sustained, sensuous articulation. The sound was originally associated with B. B. King who had called his own guitar Lucille. In deference to his hero, Clapton coined the phrase 'woman tone' for his own sound effects. These were achieved with a Gibson guitar by removing all the treble from the tone controls and turning either both pick-ups full on, or just using the rhythm pick-up.
13. Middleton and Muncie, op. cit., 79.
14. Fort, op. cit., 182.
15. However, 'whether a psychedelic song is to be defined as
    (a) a song *created* under the influence of drugs,
    (b) a song *representing* or *signifying* aspects of the drugged state, or
    (c) a song attempting to *produce* an altered state isn't always clear' (Middleton and Muncie, op. cit., 78).
16. J. Pidgeon, *Eric Clapton*, Panther, St Albans, 1976, 64.
17. Ibid., 72.
18. Marchbank, op. cit., 44.
19. Fort, op. cit., 182.
20. 'The "blue note", or "bent" and "turned" notes as blues singers sometimes call them, are essential to blues musicianship. They impart a plaintive, sometimes tense, quality to the playing which is expressive of the vocal, and made more effective by their relationship to the "true" intervals of the major scale.'
    (P. Oliver, 'Binarism, Blues and Black Culture', in R. Middleton and D. Horn, (eds), *Popular Music* 2, Cambridge University Press, Cambridge, 1982, 184).
21. Pidgeon, op. cit., 78.
22. Ibid., 62.
23. H. Brown and D. Pearce, *Jimi Hendrix*, Wise Publications, London, 1978, 13.
24. C. Gillett, *The Sound of the City*, Souvenir Press, London and Canada, 385.
25. Pidgeon, op. cit., 62.
26. To quote Richard Neville, 'The music – the usual delirious, steamy mixture of black power and masturbation' (op. cit., 38).
27. N. Jones, 'Hendrix – on the Crest of a Fave Rave', *Melody Maker,* 21 January 1967, 8.
28. The 'fuzz' effect, so important in Hendrix's music, is effectively a severe distortion. The first deliberate distortion of this type was produced in the mid-sixties by damaging the speaker cones of an amplifier system. This meant they could no longer give a true response and thus introduced some distortion. The first properly controlled fuzz was produced in much the same way as it is today, except that valves were used rather than amplifiers' transistors. The input signal from the guitar is greatly amplified to exceed the signal level above the supply voltage. As this is not possible, the signal becomes saturated at the supply voltage level. This has the effect of clipping the top of the wave form to produce the distortion.

This effect was used by rock musicians to produce the 'aggressive' quality through the introduction of many high frequency harmonies. Naturally produced sound waves have only a few harmonies, but these 'clipped' waves have many, especially at a high level and this is what gives off the piercingly painful effect. Natural guitar sounds at loud volume are not nearly so painful to listen to, and hence far less aggressive.

Hendrix took this use of fuzz much further by using amplifiers with a much higher gain. This meant that most of the signal was clipped, leaving only the bass part :

Figure 1

This greatly increased the effect by making the signal much harsher. At times he also used extremely highgain fuzz which left practically none of the original signal and the output was similar to a square wave:

Figure 2

It is probable that Hendrix later used transistors in his fuzz box. These have much higher gain than valves as they saturate faster, giving very square cut-offs as opposed to valves which tend to saturate more slowly, thus giving a more rounded and softer fuzz.

Possibly the first record to feature intentional use of controlled random feedback was 'Anyway, Anyhow, Anywhere' by The Who in May 1965. The fuzz-box was first prominently featured on the Rolling Stones' *(I Can't Get No) Satisfaction* in August of the same year. This was a distinctly different one to that Jeff Beck achieved on the Yardbirds' 'Shapes of Things' in March 1966. By the skilful combination of finger vibrato and manipulation of the gain control on the fuzz-box, he managed to make the guitar sustain almost indefinitely, almost like a sitar. The characteristics of the guitar and its pickups were vitally important in this controlled use of feedback. Beck was using a Fender Esquire, which needed this boost from the fuzz-box. Eric Clapton, on the other hand, was using a Gibson 'Les Paul', which had much more powerful pickups than the Fender Esquire and the searing, sustained sound he obtained on John Mayall's Bluesbreakers' album (July '66) owes nothing to the fuzz-box at all.

Hendrix combined all the elements mentioned above, used by Townshend, Clapton and Beck, adding many innovations of his own, including the use of the Stratocaster's tremolo arm (to bend the pitch) and wah-wah pedal (a device to control harmonics). This arsenal of sound, combined with his formidable technique and powerful stage presence account for the enormous impact he made on the pop world. I am indebted here to Keith Hale for his helpful advice and notes on fuzz-boxes.

29. The underlying beat works in a manner similar to that employed by Pink Floyd in the opening track of *Dark Side of the Moon* where the heartbeat establishes a common pulse, so creating a bonding between performer and listener.

30. In common with all genres in music, an understanding of form depends upon comparison and contrast. Its form of communication is symbolic and pre-conditioned by the structures of previous symbolic transfer. In the case of space rock, listeners could draw on their experience of the Byrds, Pink Floyd etc. In Hendrix, however, space rock is an attempt to *destroy* reality to constitute his own reality based on a sense of the anarchic (see p. 23).

31. Fort, op. cit., 182.

32. Ibid., 181, 183.

33. C. Gillett, op. cit., 385.

34. *Melody Maker*, June 1967.

35. In P. Willis, *Profane Culture*, Routledge & Kegan Paul, London, 1978.

36. Miles, *Pink Floyd*, Omnibus Press, 1980 London, 1966. As the pages are not numbered, references have been put under the month, year headings, used in the book.

37. Ibid., 11 October 1966.

38. Ibid.

39. Ibid., 23 December 1966.

40. Downing, op. cit., 95.

41. A simplified edition of the score can be found in *Pink Floyd, Two*, Hampshire House Publishing and Essex Music International, London, 1969, 1976.

42. The four-chord harmonic sequence is in itself unpredictable in that it does not follow the traditional logic of chord progressions, (e.g. use of cadences, key modulations). 'Syntactically, then, it's an idea with high originality and, in the context of "space rock", this might perhaps signify something like "exploration of new realms", "lack of firm ground or steady centre".' Middleton and Muncie, op. cit., 82.

43. The momentary key shift to F major, which is unrelated to the overall harmonic context, has a certain simple naivety when set against the hypnotic effect of the repeated cell-like phrases in the vocal on C# over the E major instrumental. The effect is one of pure colour as opposed to the palette-like mix of the surrounding chords and electronic effects.

44. While the chord sequence in itself is unusual in terms of traditional harmonic progression, its repeated use gives a sense of familiarity so that the exploration of space (as connoted by the pre-recorded effects, improvisation and electronic noise) is 'controlled' by Floyd. By forming the background of the piece, 'the joins between statements [are] disguised, links, introductions and codas added, so that the music seems to flow on continuously' (Middleton and Muncie, op. cit., 82).

45. The use of a perfect cadence after the somewhat unpredictable chord progressions effects a sense of traditional closure, a landing back on Earth after an exploration of space.

46. Miles, op. cit., 30 April 1967.

47. Neville, op. cit., 28.

48. Miles, op. cit., 21 September 1967.

49. Barrett composed and performed on only one track of *A Saucerful of Secrets* (*Jugband Blues*). Subsequently he made one single and two solo albums, *The Madcap Laughs* (1970) and *Barrett* (1970). *Syd Barrett* (1974) was a re-issue of these.

50. Miles, op. cit., September/October 1970.

51. Middleton and Muncie, op. cit., 78.

52. This accounts in some way for the attraction for counter-culture of the world views of dispossessed subcultural groups.

53. Underground musicians, both in England the States, were initially against recording and commercialism. Arthur Brown and Country Joe and the Fish, for example, refused to release recordings as they felt that these would compromise their stand against capitalism.

54. Analysed in Chapter 3 of this book.

55. Gillett, op. cit., 375.

56. Pidgeon, op. cit., 72.
Grateful acknowledgment is made to Pete Winkler, State University of New York, Stonybrook, for his help in transcribing *Purple Haze* and *Love or Confusion*, and to Helen Moulton for her helpful suggestions.

3 THE BEATLES

1. William Mann, music critic of *The Times*, in D. Taylor, *It Was Twenty Years Ago Today*, Bantam Press, London 45.
2. D. Taylor, *As Time Goes By*, Abacus, London, 1974, 55.
3. R. Goldstein, 'I Blew My Cool Through the New York Times', *New Times and the Village Voice*, 1967, 173/4.
4. In Taylor, *It Was Twenty Years Ago Today,* op. cit., 45.
5. Ibid., 45.
6. Goldstein, op. cit., 175.
7. Cream: *I Feel Free,* January 1967;
   Pink Floyd: *Arnold Layne,* April 1967;
               See Emily Play, July/August 1967;
   Jimi Hendrix: *Hey Joe,* January/February 1967;
               Purple Haze, April/June 1967;
               The Wind Cries Mary, June 1967.
8. T. Leary, *Time Out*, 873, (13–29 May 1987), 19.
9. Miles, *Pink Floyd*, Omnibus Press, London 1980, 23 December, 1966 (references are to the month and year headings used in the book).

   Paul McCartney had also been a regular visitor to Spontaneous Underground, which promised nothing in the way of entertainment only; 'costume, masque, ethnic, space, Edwardian, Victorian and hipness – generally . . . face and body makeup – certainly' (ibid., 1966).
10. Ibid., 11 October 1966.
11. R. Neville, *Play Power*, Jonathan Cape, London, 1970, 24.
12. C. Gillett, *The Sound of the City*, Souvenir Press, London, 1970, 264.
13. Ibid., 266.
14. 'He regards himself as still primarily an instrumentalist. Who, on hearing that voice, could dissent from that view? He admits that he finds the singing difficult. "Singing with the boys used to be easy, because John used to take me through the lyric. I'd stand there, thinking I was Stevie Wonder: then I'd go in the control box and find out I was Bing Crosby. I've got a lot more confident, but I can still feel it shaking" – he pulled at his Adam's apple – "in here. I've got the range of the common housewife." . . . It was only in America where instrumentalists are valued that he was given equal billing with John, George and Paul' (P. Norman, 'Ringo: a Starr is Bored', in *The Road Goes on Forever*, Corgi Books, London 1982, 80).
15. J. Fort, *The Pleasure Seekers: The Drug Crisis, Youth and Society*, Grove Press, New York, 1969, 130.
16. Ibid., 131.
17. I. Whitcomb, *Rock Odyssey: A Chronicle of the Sixties*, Hutchinson, London, 1984, 251.
18. The publicity attending the Beatles' one-page ad supporting the legalisation of marijuana and their two earlier psychedelic singles helps to construct an image of the 'knowledgeable guide'. Lucy furthers the experience by showing the positive aspects of a trip – the colour and beauty of the experience. See also Fort, op. cit., 136.
19. R. Middleton and J. Muncie, 'Pop Culture and Post-war Youth: Countercultures', in *Popular Culture*, Open University Press, Milton Keynes, 1981, 79.
20. W. Mellers, *Twilight of the Gods: The Beatles in Retrospect*, Faber & Faber, London, 1973, 89.
21. Neville, op. cit., 79.
22. Middleton and Muncie, op. cit., 79.

23. P. McCabe and R. D. Schonfield, *Apple to the Core: The Unmaking of the Beatles*, Martin Brian & O'Keefe, London, 1972, 81–2.
24. Ibid., 82.
25. Ibid.
26. Ibid., 84.
27. Ibid., 80.
28. Ibid., 85.
29. Ibid.
30. 'Blurred, overlapping timbres, often filtered of some of their constituent filters to produce "empty" blank sounds [and] bright, tinkly sounds (such as the harpsichord)' were often used to represent hallucinatory conditions, the blurred images and speech and unnaturally bright colours (Middleton and Muncie, op. cit., 79).
31. 'Pop culture today is probably for the first time determined by youth who, with folk-rock, acid-rock, raga-rock, light shows, poster art and the psychedelic scene in general, have determined the cultural values for society.

    'Many heroes come from such imaginative and absurdly titled groups as Big Brother and the Holding Company, the Grateful Dead, the Quicksilver Messenger Service, the Fugs, Buffalo Springfield, the Mothers of Invention, the Peanutbutter Conspiracy, the Byrds, the Rolling Stones, the Beatles, Country Joe and the Fish, Jefferson Airplane and Bob Dylan. The Beatles' albums *Sgt. Pepper's Lonely Hearts Club Band* and *Revolver* have numerous songs with drug themes, and there are also *Let's Get Stoned, Rainy Day Woman, Eight Miles High, Hey, Mr. Tambourine Man, Can't Get High, Flying High, Mind Gardens, Lucy in the Sky with Diamonds, A Little Help From My Friends, Mother's Little Helper, Connection, Crystal Ship* and many others.

    'The records listened to incessantly include the following words (warily listened to by the older generation who usually hear only the music while complaining of its loudness': "There's something happening here. What it is ain't exactly clear. There is a man with a gun over there telling me I've got to beware. I think it's time we stopped. Children what's that sound. Everyone look what's going down," (Buffalo Springfield). "Mr. America, walk on by your supermarket dream, Mr. America, walk on by the liquor store supreme, Mr. America, try and hide the emptiness that's you inside' (The Mothers of Invention); 'And you ask me why I don't live here, hey, how come you have to ask me that?' (Bob Dylan); 'All the lonely people, where do they all belong ?' (The Beatles); 'He's as blind as he can be, just sees what he wants to see, nowhere man, can you see me at all?' (The Beatles); 'Slow down, you move too fast, you've got to make the morning last' (Simon and Garfunkel); 'All I want is just be free and live my life the way I want it to be. All I want is to just have fun and live my life like it just begun. But you're pushing too hard on me' (The Seeds); 'Come Mothers and Fathers throughout the land, and don't criticise what you can't understand. Your sons and your daughters are beyond your command. Your old road is rapidly aging . . . The times they are a'changing' (Bob Dylan); 'All you need is love, love is all you need' (The Beatles) (Fort, op. cit., 211–12).
32. R. Poirier, 'Learning from the Beatles', in J. Eisen, (ed.) *The Age of Rock*, Vintage Books, New York, 1969, 174.
33. Ibid, 173–4.
34. J. Norman, 'I Was Never Lovable: I Was Just Lennon', in Norman, op. cit., 32.
35. Neville, op. cit., 116.
36. Ibid., 225–8.
37. Ibid., 223–4.
38. The key note, or first note of the scale, has strong connotations of home-centredness. In classical music, there is generally a move away, either to the dominant (fifth) or relative minor, accompanied by a return to give a traditional

   A:B:A: structure. This pulls on the sense of 'home-centredness' referred to by
   Fort, op. cit., 131–2.
39. Fort, op. cit., 182–3.
40. Ibid., 183.
41. McCabe and Schonfield, op. cit., 80.
42. Neville, op. cit., 53.
43. Ibid.
44. The dominant (fifth) generates a strong sense of movement back to the tonic, or
    home key.
45. A plagal cadence (IV–I) is used for the 'Amen' (surely, so let it be) in liturgical
    composition.
46. Neville, op. cit., 116.
47. Miles, op. cit., 23 December 1966.
48. Neville, op. cit., 24.
49. Ibid.
50. Ibid., 114, 101.
51. Mellers, op. cit., 94.
52. Poirier, op. cit., 174–5.
53. Neville, op. cit., 173.
54. Fort, op. cit., 15–16.
55. C. Belz, *The Story of Rock*, Oxford University Press, New York, 1969, 169.
56. If musical structures that suggest hallucinogenic experience are characterised by
    a conjunction of electronically manipulated blurred and overlapping timbres,
    irregular rhythms and lurching harmonics, then the clarity of line, texture and
    rhythm in *When I'm Sixty-Four* would suggest the opposite, an experience
    strongly based in the *real* world.
57. Mellers, op. cit.
58. Ibid.
59. M. Wood, 'Arts in Society: John Lennon's School Days', in Eisen, op. cit., 121.
60. In particular the 'earth mother' stereotype.
61. J. Peyser, 'The Beatles and the Beatless', in Eisen, op. cit., 132.
62. Neville, op. cit., 79. The quote continues: 'in 1967 a new sort of music showed us
    Strawberry Fields Forever – it was nicknamed acid rock, after the famous
    Monterey Festival, and then instantly internationalised with the release of the
    Beatles' *Sergeant Pepper*. Acid rock was flower power's jingle.'
63. Middleton and Muncie, op. cit., 88.
64. Mellers, op. cit., 96.
65. P. E. Willis, *Profane Culture*, Routledge & Kegan Paul, London, 1978.
66. While the musical coding of *A Day in the Life* is ambiguous, Joan Peyser's
    interpretation does suggest a finality which is focused on the duration of the final
    chord: 'the unpitched sounds return, increase in volume and duration until they
    dissolve, with suddenness into one resonant, depressing, seemingly interminable
    terminal tonic chord' (Eisen, op. cit.).
67. Neville, op. cit., 116: 'LSD transforms the mundane into the sensational. This
    applies to sounds, smells, colours, tastes, touch, everyday experiences.'
68. Ibid., 116.
69. Ibid., 115.
70. Mellers, op. cit., 98.
71. Poirier, op. cit., 176.
72. Neville, op. cit., 99.
73. G. Marcus, 'The Beatles' in J. Miller, (ed.), *The Rolling Stone Illustrated
    History of Rock and Roll*, Random House, New York, 1976, 175.
74. Leary, op. cit., 19.
75. McCabe and Schonfield, op. cit., 86–7.

76. A. Shaw, *The Rock Revolution*, Collier-Macmillan, London, 1969, 81.
77. R. Connolly, *The Beatles Complete*, Northern Songs, Introduction.
78. Shaw, op. cit., 80–1.
79. Miles, op. cit., 21 September 1967.
80. C. Schofield, *Jagger*, Methuen, London, 1983, 130.
81. N. Logan, and B. Wooffinden, *The Illustrated Encyclopaedia of Rock*, Salamander Books, London, 1976, 25.
82. Mellers, op. cit., 146.
83. T. Roszak, *The Making of a Counter-Culture: Reflections on the Technocratic Society and its Youthful Opposition*, Faber & Faber, London, 1970, 82–3.
84. Ibid., 156.
85. There is a similar alliance in *Tomorrow Never Knows*. While this is an earlier hallucinogenic track (1966), Lennon had originally imagined 'that in the background you would hear thousands of monks chanting, that was impractical of course, and we did something different. I should have tried to get near my original idea, the monks singing, I realise now that was what I wanted' (*The Beatles Complete*, op. cit.).

4 1967 AND PSYCHEDELIC ROCK

1. On the relationship of psychedelic drugs to sexual desire see J. Fort, *The Pleasure Seekers: The Drug Crisis, Youth and Society*, Grove Press, New York, 1969, 138.
2. See Chapters 3 and 5.
3. T. Jasper, *British Record Charts, 1955–1978*, Macdonald and Jane's, London, 1978, 128–37.
4. Fort, op. cit., 210.
5. While the subject of protest/revolution appears consistently in the early recordings of Bob Dylan, Joan Baez, Phil Ochs, Tom Paxton and Pete Seeger and in songs by Crosby, Stills and Nash, the Doors, Creedence Clearwater, Country Joe McDonald, the Lovin' Spoonful, Peter, Paul and Mary, the Byrds and Leonard Cohen, there are only a few songs by British artists. Those considered 'definitive' in *The Rock Music Source Book* are: *We Can Change the World, Songs for Beginners*, Graham Nash; *Power to the People, Shaved Fish*, John Lennon; *Revolution, The Beatles (White Album), The Beatles 1967–70; Won't Get Fooled Again, Who's Next, The Kids Are Alright*, The Who; *The Laws Must Change, The Turning Point*, John Mayall; *Let's Burn Down Cornfields, It Ain't Easy*, Long John Baldry. The majority were released post-1967. (B. Macken, P. Fornatale and B. Ayres, *The Rock Music Source Book*, Anchor Books, New York, 1980, 317–24).
6. R. Middleton and J. Muncie, 'Pop Culture, Pop Music and Post-War Youth: Counter-cultures', in *Politics, Ideology and Popular Culture*, Open University Press, Milton Keynes, 1981, 87.
7. Bob Dylan, *Mr. Tambourine Man*; The Byrds, *Eight Miles High*; Pete Seeger, *Mayrowana*; Bette Midler, Country Joe and the Fish, *Marijuana*; The Stones, *Mother's Little Helper*; The Beach Boys, *Good Vibrations*; The Beatles, *Yellow Submarine*; The Mindbenders, *A Groovy Kind of Love*; Donovan, *Sunshine Superman*.
8. C. Gillett, *The Sound of the City*, Souvenir Press, London, 1970, 353.
9. Ibid., 352.
10. R. Neville, *Play Power*, Paladin, London, 1971, 28.
11. Gillett, op. cit., 354.
12. Fort, op. cit., 220.

13. Miles, *Pink Floyd*, Omnibus Press, London 1980. References are to the month and year headings used in this book.

14. Ibid., 27 March 1966.

15. J. Nuttall, *Bomb Culture*, London, Paladin, 1970, 210.

16. Ibid., 211.

17. T. McGrath, *International Times*, 10, 13 March 1967.

18. G. Melly, *Revolt into Style*, Allen Lane, The Penguin Press, London 1979, 116.

19. Guidance by a trained, trusted person is an important factor, and dosage is a more important variable than with other drugs. With an average dose the effects begin within 30–45 minutes and usually last 8–12 hours. Mild physical sensations, particularly in the limbs, occur, but the main dimensions of the drug reaction are perceptual, cognitive (thought), and affective (mood). See Fort, op. cit., 182.

20. See Chapter 3, The Beatles.

21. See Fort, op. cit., 181–2.

22. Melly, op. cit., 110.

23. N. Logan and B. Wooffinden, *The Illustrated Encyclopaedia of Rock*, Salamandar Books, London, 1976, 68.

24. *Season of the Witch* (1966 and 1967), *Mellow Yellow* (1966).

25. N. Cohn, *Awopbopaloobop Alopbamboom: Pop From the Beginning*, Paladin, London, 1972, 179.

26. Middleton and Muncie, op. cit., 85.

27. 'Intergalactic Union', *Dopogram, Evo*, 24 March 1970.

28. See Chapter 3, for analysis.

29. Fort, op. cit., 187.

30. Miles, op. cit., 1966.

31. Logan and Wooffinden, op. cit., 165.

32. Reissued in June 1972, the song did not achieve anything like its previous success.

33. There is a certain homology with R.D. Laing's definition of the goal of 'true sanity': 'in one way or another, the dissolution of the normal ego . . . competently adjusted to our alienated social reality; the emergence of the "inner" archetypal, mediators of divine power, and through this death a rebirth, and the eventual re-establishment of a new kind of ego-functioning, the ego now being the servant of the divine, no longer its betrayer' (R.D. Laing, *The Politics of Experience and The Bird of Paradise*, Penguin Books, London, 1967, 119).

The questioning of 'reason' and 'reality' in *A Whiter Shade of Pale* attacks 'men at the very core of their security by denying the validity of everything they mean when they utter the most precious word in their vocabulary: the word "I". And yet this is what the counter-culture undertakes when, by way of its mystical tendencies or the drug experience, it assaults the reality of the ego as an isolable, purely cerebral unit of identity.' (T. Roszak, *The Making of a Counter Culture: Reflections on the Technocratic Society and its Youthful Opposition*, Faber & Faber, London, 1971, 55).

At the same time, it evokes McGrath's observation on the counter-culture's construction of an alternative society which 'operates in different conceptions of time and space'. See (McGrath, op. cit.).

34. Considered by Landau to be the criteria of art in rock. (S. Frith, 'Rock and Popular Culture', *Socialist Revolution*, 31 (1977), 15).

35. Neville, op. cit., 79.

36. The constant repetition of two chords works, in some ways, like a tape loop. You only know where you are if you remember the initial sequence. This creates a sense of timelessness.

37. Melisma: a group of notes sung to one syllable.

38. Fort, op. cit., 182–3.
39. For discussion of *Purple Haze* see pp. 17–22.
40. Marijuana is a much gentler drug, originally called 'Giver of Delight', 'The Heavenly Guide', or 'Paradise' (normally associated with a beautiful woman).
41. Estimates by various writers and spokesmen on marijuana vary from one million to twelve million current [1969] users. (Fort, op. cit., 29).
42. Fort, op. cit., 182–3.
43. For example distancing of vocal, bright tinkly sounds, blurred overlapping timbres.
44. Neville, op. cit., 78.
45. Miles, op. cit., 11 March 1967.
46. Ibid., 12 May 1967.
47. Jasper, op. cit., 132.
48. Miles, op. cit., 1966.
49. See Neville, op. cit., 'The Politics of Play', 204–88.
50. The original repetition of the tonic note (I) firmly establishes a sense of key. Traditionally, the song would have ended on a V–I cadence, so confirming the key and providing a sense of finality. By ending on a V–1 (imperfect cadence) there is a sense of incompletion.
51. Jasper, op. cit., 132.
52. The song was adapted from *Lawdy Mamma* and was a stated tribute to Albert King. The solo, in particular, has an uncanny resemblance to King's own *Crosscut Saw*.
53. P. McCabe and R.D. Schonfield, *Apple to the Core: The Unmaking of the Beatles*, Martin Brian & O'Keefe, London, 1972, 82.
54. Neville, op. cit., 24.
55. D. Taylor, *As Time Goes By*, Abacus/Shlere, 1974, 55.
56. C. Belz, *The Story of Rock*, Oxford University Press, New York, 1969, 149.
57. See Chapter 3.
58. Occasionally users of LSD experience perceptual changes (delayed onset) months or even years after taking the drug.
59. Jasper, op. cit., 133.
60. Gillett, op. cit., 268.
61. See Chapter 5.
62. S. Booth, 'The True Adventures of the Rolling Stones', in B. Burford, (ed.), *Granta*, Penguin Books, Harmondsworth, 1984, 12.
63. Logan and Wooffinden, op. cit., 197.
64. McCabe and Schonfield, op. cit., 82.
65. R. Christgau, 'The Rolling Stones', in J. Miller (ed.), *Rolling Stone Illustrated History of Rock and Roll*, Random House, New York, 1976, 182.
66. Jasper, op. cit., 133.
67. Ibid.
68. Neville, op. cit., 31.
69. With the exception of *Dark Side of the Moon*, No. 6, Best Selling Albums, 1973; No. 5, 1974; No. 19, 1975 (Jasper, op. cit.)
70. R.J. Gleason, 'Like a Rolling Stone', in J. Eisen, (ed.), *The Age of Rock*, Vintage Books, New York, 1969, 72.
71. Middleton and Muncie, op. cit., 87.
72. P. Willis, *Profane Culture*, Routledge & Kegan Paul, London, 1978.
73. Ibid.
74. Ibid.
75. See Chapter 3.
76. Neville, op. cit., 30.
77. Ibid., 35–8.

78. Middleton and Muncie, op. cit., 87.
79. Roszak, op. cit., 156.

5 THE ROLLING STONES

1. P. Willis, 'The Creative Age', in *Profane Culture*, Routledge & Kegan Paul, London, 1978.
2. *Oz*, July 1968.
3. This combination of tribal unity and egocentricity is possibly the reason why the impression of mass sexual energy can produce an unpleasant feeling of auto-eroticism, self-gratification and mass masturbation. Tony Palmer comments: '[The Stones' music] had the guilty throb of lust, with no expectation of pleasure and the hope of satisfaction. It was irresistible, certainly, but also gloating and secret. It communicated nothing but the closedness of the adolescent nightmares which were paraded before us by way of truth, and nothing but the debauchery and gluttony of indiscipline' (T. Palmer, *Born Under a Bad Sign*, William Kimber, London, 1970, 76).

   Musically, this is reflected in the movement from the more unselfconscious egotism of barrelhouse to the more conscious egotism and sexual display which accompanied rock 'n' roll and r&b.
4. Underground manifestos stressed the following:

   (a) the spread of an ego-dissolving delirium wherein a tribal telepathic understanding could grow up among men.
   (b) To re-ignite an overwhelming sense of wonderment at the Universe, to cultivate aesthetic perception in the face of utilitarian perception, to reinstate the metalled road as a silken ribbon and the hydraulic waterfall as a galaxy of light.
   (c) To expand the range of human consciousness outside the continuing and ultimately soul-destroying boundaries of the political/utilitarian frame of reference.
   (d) To institute an international tribe or class outside the destructive system of the nations.
   (e) To outflank police, educationists and moralists through whom the death machine was/is maintained.
   (f) To release forces into the prevailing culture that would dislocate society, untie its stabilizing knots of morality, punctuality, servility and property.
   (g) To institute a sense of festivity into public life whereby people could fuck freely and guiltlessly, dance wildly and wear fancy dress all the time.
   (h) To eradicate utterly and forever the Pauline lie implicit in Christian convention, that people neither shit, piss nor fuck. To set up a common public idea of what a human being is that retains its sense of health and beauty pertaining to the genitals and the arsehole.
                                    (J. Nuttall, *Bomb Culture*, London, 1970, 249).

5. The second half of the sixties saw an escalation in student protest and rebellion in most of the industrially developed countries including Japan. Influenced by the ideas of Marx, Lenin, Guevara and Marcuse, students and intellectuals aimed at the destruction of capitalism to make a world free from war, poverty and exploitation. Mass student revolt started in the United States, the prototype being the 1964 Free Speech Movement at Berkeley, part of the University of California. Over the next four years dissent and student revolt against the educational and social system increased across the US culminating in 221 major upheavals in 101 campuses in the six months up to June 1968.

Students in Europe were greatly influenced by radical protest in the US, the main difference being that they were more ideological, mixing Marx with a good dash of anarchism, especially in France and Germany.

6. Tom McGrath wrote the following in *IT*: 'It is essentially an inner-directed movement. Those involved in it share a common viewpoint – a new way of looking at things – [which has supplanted] credo, dogma or ideology. This can never be suppressed by force or Law: you cannot imprison consciousness. No matter how many raids and arrests the police make on whatever pretence – there can be no final bust because the revolution has taken place WITHIN THE MINDS OF THE YOUNG' (Nuttall, op. cit., 214).

Roszak also draws attention to consciousness: 'Perhaps the young of this generation haven't the stamina to launch the epochal transformation they seek; but there should be no mistaking the fact that they want nothing less. "Total rejection" is a phrase that comes readily to their lips, often before the mind provides even a blurred picture of the new culture that is to displace the old. If there is anything about the ethos of Black Power that proves particularly attractive to young white disaffiliates who cannot gain access to the movement, it is the sense that Black Power somehow implies an entirely new way of life: a black culture, a black consciousness' (T. Roszak, *The Making of a Counter Culture: Reflections on the Technocratic Society and its Youthful Opposition*, Faber & Faber, London, 1970, 44).

7. Ibid., 66.

8. Other groups also assumed ambiguous and enigmatic names: Big Brother and the Holding Company, Quicksilver Messenger Service, Buffalo Springfield, the Mothers of Invention, the Peanut Butter Conspiracy, Jefferson Airplane, etc. *Trout Mask Replica* (Captain Beefheart and His Magic Band) points to the enigmatic stance of the band, and this also comes through in the ambiguities of self-identity, e.g. Mr Zoot Horn Rollo.

In many ways this masking of identity parallels the notions contained in R.D. Laing, *The Divided Self* (Penguin, Harmondsworth, 1990), where the extent of fissure at the subjective level is explored from an existential anti-mainstream psychiatric background.

9. R. Neville, *Play Power*, Paladin, London, 1971, 75.

10. Ibid., 116.

11. J. Fort, *The Pleasure Seekers: The Drug Crisis, Youth and Society*, Grove Press, New York, 1969, 183.

12. See discussion on Charles Manson and the Family, pp. 100–102.

13. *Helix*, Seattle, July 1967.

14. 'While the cultivation of a feminine softness . . . is the occasion of endless satire on the part of critics . . . the style is clearly a deliberate effort on the part of the young to undercut the crude and compulsive he-manliness of American political life. While this generous and gentle eroticism is available to us, we would do well to respect it, instead of ridiculing it' (Roszak, op. cit., 74).

15. Neville, op. cit., 64.

16. 'Play is Fun. Play is Freedom' and 'Sex is Pure when it's Playful' (Ibid., 222–5).

17. Roszak, op. cit., 75.

18. Cited ibid., 97. For Marx it was 'not the consciousness of men that determines their social being, but, on the contrary, their social being that determines their consciousness'. However, as Roszak points out, it was a thesis 'which never quite managed to account for Karl Marx himself and the bourgeois intellectual defectors he expected to take leadership of the proletariat' (ibid.).

19. Ibid., 107.

20. Ibid., 115.

21. The atrocities started more or less accidentally once Zappa's group, the Mothers

of Invention, were well-established. When the anti-Vietnam movement was at its height, Zappa invited some uniformed US Marines on stage during a show. He gave them a life-size doll, saying, 'This is a gook baby, show us how we treat gooks in Vietnam.' The Marines, who rose to the occasion, tore the doll, stuffed limb from stuffed limb. 'After that,' says Zappa, 'we included props in all our shows. I call them visual aids.' (From *Rock 'n' Roll Babylon* by Gary Herman, Plexus, London, 1982).

Frank Zappa's attempt to provide an anti-war ethic does suggest a particularly apposite and articulate philosophy. However, it is apparent that theatrical gestures can misfire and whilst the mutilation of a life-size doll can be interpreted as an anti-war statement, it cannot be assumed that an audience will always decode accurately, as current research on audience behaviour would confirm.

22. 'The mood is right for us to fight politics with music, because rock is now a media. Sure it's basically recreation but because we've now applied new rules to the way it's run, it's also a weapon. Let's use it' (*IT*, 56, 1969).

23. Neville, op. cit., 69.

24. P. Wicke, 'Rock Music: A Musical Aesthetic Study', in R. Middleton and D. Horn, *Popular Music, 2. Theory and Method*, Cambridge University Press, Cambridge, 1982, 239.

25. Zappa was generally very theatrical, persuading marines on one occasion to break up dolls on stage to reinforce his stand against war and in particular Vietnam. He also supported the Plaster Caster of Chicago, who immortalised pop stars' penises in plaster of paris. 'I appreciate what they're doing,' said Frank Zappa, both artistically and sociologically. Sociologically it's really heavy.' Cynthia Plaster Caster concurred. 'I think every girl should be a plaster caster – try it at least once. It's going to be a significant element in the revolution' (*Ann Arbor Argus*, April 1969. From an interview recorded while Cynthia was in Ann Arbor, Michigan, to cast MC5).

26. Roszak, op. cit., 75.

27. S. Frith, 'Rock and Popular Culture', *Radical Philosophy*, 103, Radical Philosophy Group, Mathematics Faculty, Open University, Milton Keynes.

28. *Rock 'n' Roll Babylon*, Gary Herman, Plexus, London, 1982, 113.

29. This preoccupation with alienation also comes through in *I Can't Explain*, by The Who.

30. Booth, op. cit., 42.

31. This is personified in Jagger's 'Mr Turner' in the movie *Performance* (1970). Turner lives in an upstairs flat, surrounded by beautiful women, musical instruments and drugs, and is virtually cut off from the outside world. In many ways, this reflects the attempt by the counter-culture to establish on a mass scale the lifestyle of the 'outsider' as defined in H. Becker's classic text on deviance (*The Outsider*, Becker, Free Press, United States, 1963; an examination of the lives of jazz musicians in the early sixties).

32. R. Christgau, 'The Rolling Stones', in N. Logan and B. Wooffinden, *Illustrated Encyclopedia of Rock*, Salamander Books, London, 1976, 187.

33. F. Newman, 'I used to Think I Was Really Ugly', in J. Eisen (ed.), *The Age of Rock*, New York, 1969, 105.

34. N. Cohn, *Awopbopaloobop Alopbamboom: Pop from the Beginning*, London, 1969, 147.

35. C. Gillett, *The Sound of the City*, Souvenir Press, London, 1970, 268.

36. R. Merton, 'Comment' on the Stones, in Eisen, op. cit., 116.

37. The Stones' return to their r&b based style in *Jumpin' Jack Flash* and *Street Fighting Man* would appear to bear this out. By the early seventies The Stones confirmed their position at the centre of popular music with their aptly named single, *Exile on Main Street*.

38. Roszak, op. cit., 14.
39. For example in *Mother's Little Helper, Satisfaction, Going Home, Paint It Black, Under My Thumb, Stupid Girl, Back Street Girl, Yesterday's Papers.*
40. See Chapter 3, pp. 49–50.

41. 'My dear Lady Anne
I've done what I can
I must take my leave
For promised I am
This play is run, my love,
Your time has come, my love,
I've pledged my troth to Lady Jane

Oh, my sweet Marie
I wait at your ease
The sands have run out
For your lady and me
Wedlock is nigh my love
Her station's right my love
Life is secure with Lady Jane.

42. See, for example, *A Whiter Shade of Pale.*
43. See Chapter 3.
44. Fort, op. cit., 20.
45. P. Oliver, *Conversations with the Blues*, London, 1965, 23.
46. In *Spanish Castle Magic*, for example, the use of noise shuts off the real world, the speed of the music providing a metaphor for the 'speed' connotations of acids – 'Just float your little mind around'. The endless feedback and distortion move the listener into an equivalent state of incoherence – the montage of sound effects resonating with the kaleidoscopic images: 'And the Wind's just right. Hang on my darling.'
47. E.g. the setting of a 'lonely hearts club' to solve the problems of the alienated in society.
48. Cohn, op. cit., 147.
49. Palmer, op. cit., 76.
50. *Paint it Black, Get Off Of My Cloud* are also closer to the aggressive mood.
51. There are also parallels with such extreme bands as MC5, The Fugs, Love, The Grateful Dead. It has also been recorded that Manson himself saw the inspiration for much of his philosophy in the Beatles *Piggies.*
52. S. Ewen, *Charles Manson and the Family*, CCCS Occasional Paper, 35.
53. Ibid., 36.
54. Ibid., 36.
55. Ibid., 36.
56. Ibid., 38.
57. For example, Los Angeles, Oaklands, Belfast, The Hague, New Brighton, Ipswich (1964–7).
58. Booth, op. cit., 92.
59. Ewen, op. cit., 38.
60. See Booth, op. cit., 80–3.

6 PINK FLOYD: *DARK SIDE OF THE MOON*

1. Manson was the most highly publicised example of the adverse effects of LSD. His influence extended to the Beach Boys. Prior to the release of their 1969

album *20/20* the group had released a love song called *Never Learn Not To Love*. On one level it cajoles 'give up your ego and let's fuck', and beneath that 'give up your world and join mine for the sake of true love'. The song had been written by Charles Manson. Manson was not the only Family member to be patronised by Dennis Wilson. In 1967 a full-page ad. was run in the *Village Voice* stating 'In Memoriam Kenneth Anger'. This was not a death announcement but a renouncement of film-making after Bobby Beausoleil, the original Lucifer actor in Anger's movie *Lucifer Rising* had stolen 1600 feet of the picture and taken it to Manson. Beausoleil became embroiled in The Family and was subsequently convicted of the murder of Gary Hinman. His musical abilities came to the fore in death row where he recorded a soundtrack for *Lucifer Rising*. Others to contribute soundtracks included Mick Jagger and Jimmy Page. See also Chapter 5.

2. 'James Taylor: One Man's Family of Rock', *Time*, 31 March 1971, 35.
3. The panic reactions and disorientation caused by LSD can be particularly acute if the user is placed in a jail or hospital emergency waiting room. (J. Fort, *The Pleasure Seekers: The Drug Crisis, Youth and Society*, Grove Press, New York, 1969, 132).
4. The effect is similar to that of a tape loop: after even a short period of time there is no memory of what is the beginning, what is the end.
5. See Chapter 2, *Astronomy Dominé, Set the Controls for the heart of the Sun*, and *Echoes*.
6. R. Neville, *Play Power*, Paladin, London, 1971, 14.
7. R. Middleton and J. Muncie, 'Pop Culture, Pop Music and Post-war youth: Counter-Cultures', in *Popular Culture*, Open University Press, Milton Keynes, 1981, 76. See also Chapter 2.
8. See Chapters 3 and 5.
9. S. Frith, *Sociology of Rock*, Constable, London, 1978, 103, 202.
10. T. Palmer, *Born Under A Bad Sign*, Kimber, 1970, 11. As such it anticipates the Floyd's 1979 album, *The Wall*.
12. See note 4.
13. This could refer either to Barrett or to the Floyd's roadie, Roger the Hat.
14. Miles, *Pink Floyd*, Omnibus Press, London, 1980, 14 November 1967.
15. Middleton and Muncie, op. cit., 74.
16. T. Roszak, *The Making of a Counter Culture: Reflections on the Technocratic Society and Its Youthful Opposition*, Faber & Faber, London, 1970.

Index

Where a quotation is given in musical notation, the page reference is shown in bold type.